Choosing to Know Christ

MW00490933

Choosing to Know Christ

OUR ROLES IN
THE PLAN OF SALVATION

ESTER RASBAND

CFI
An imprint of Cedar Fort, Inc.
Springville, Utah

© 2020 Ester Rasband
All rights reserved.

No part of this book may be reproduced in any form whatsoever, whether by graphic, visual, electronic, film, microfilm, tape recording, or any other means, without prior written permission of the publisher, except in the case of brief passages embodied in critical reviews and articles.

This is not an official publication of The Church of Jesus Christ of Latter-day Saints. The opinions and views expressed herein belong solely to the author and do not necessarily represent the opinions or views of Cedar Fort, Inc. Permission for the use of sources, graphics, and photos is also solely the responsibility of the author.

ISBN 13: 978-1-4621-3766-4

Published by CFI, an imprint of Cedar Fort, Inc.
2373 W. 700 S., Springville, UT 84663
Distributed by Cedar Fort, Inc., www.cedarfort.com

Library of Congress Control Number: 2020931701

Cover design by Shawnda T. Craig
Cover design © 2020 Cedar Fort, Inc.

Printed in the United States of America

10 9 8 7 6 5 4 3 2 1

Printed on acid-free paper

*T*his book is dedicated to those who have made covenants and are becoming sons and daughters of Christ by loving enough to know Him.

It is also dedicated to my great-granddaughters: Virginia and Pippa Rushforth, Claire Rasband, and Baby Girl Hillier. It is my prayer that they will have that joy.

*M*any score and millennia ago, our Father brought forth on this planet, a population—conceived in liberty in order that our choices would determine our destiny and dedicated to the truth that all men are children of God, with all the responsibility and potential that implies.

Now we are engaged in a great fallen world, to see if that population, or any population so conceived and so dedicated, can develop into people who can endure perfect love for eternity.

We will little note nor long remember the pain of the suffering we have known here, but what we choose here will live forever in the hearts of our God and ourselves.

—Ester Rasband
(Thank you, Mr. Lincoln)

CONTENTS

— ⨯◦⨯ —

A PERSONAL INTRODUCTION 1

PART 1: THE REASON I'M HERE: TO CHOOSE

Chapter 1 The Attributes of Godliness 7
Chapter 2 Nurturing 17
Chapter 3 Destination Orientation 23
Chapter 4 Stewardship and Critical Mass 29
Chapter 5 Where Your Heart Is, There Will Your Treasure
Be Also 35

PART 2: BARRIERS TO THE BEST CHOICES

Chapter 6 Visibility—A Tough Sacrifice 45
Chapter 7 Eye Single vs. Having It All 53
Chapter 8 Men Are from Earth (And So Are Women) 59
Chapter 9 Thou Shalt Not Covet Another's Role 67
Chapter 10 The Power of Control vs. the Power of Influence . . . 75

PART 3: THE FULNESS OF JOY POTENTIAL

Chapter 11 Sons of Adam and Daughters of Eve 87
Chapter 12 Joy in Oneness: The Critical Mass of Love 95
Chapter 13 A Glimpse 101
Chapter 14 A Savior Has Been Provided for Us 103

ABOUT THE AUTHOR 107

A Personal Introduction

I believe with all my being that this is the most important of my books. I do realize that I say nothing new here and that "important" is a presumptuous word to use. Still, testimonies of ancient truths *are* important to bear, and this book *is* a testimony of ancient truths.

This book is, therefore, about *choosing*. That is because bearing testimony is a look into our hearts to understand the choices that have brought experience. That is how conviction comes to be, and we want to bear testimony because of our conviction. Or, as Alma might say it: we want to share with the world how the seed has expanded in our soul.[1]

A look into our own hearts can only yield an honest testimony when it is a hard look at those choices and those experiences. It's not easy to acknowledge that choices are being constantly made. We must seek to recognize *that* we are choosing and *what* we are choosing.

One of the missions I have been given in this life is to teach the doctrines of the kingdom. My great hope (albeit ambitious) is that I can help men and women understand the gospel as it applies to their roles. I tend to focus more on women, because that has become the issue of our day. But all need to understand *tha*t they are choosing and *what* they are choosing.

The understanding that has expanded in my soul has been much slower in me than I would have hoped. It is that understanding of choice making that I needed. I had thought it was all about a "common sense" look at the issues. I was filled with trust in my natural man and the automatic direction it took me.

Before I was married, I was an administrative assistant to a Washington State Congressman, and I was fascinated with my work. I still love politics. Then I married a young man who had just finished medical school. We left my delightful and remunerative job to go where he could finish his training. I confess that it was not a difficult choice. He was worth it, and I never considered otherwise.

---

1. See Alma 32.

I was employed in the new location, but with much less money and infinitely less interest. While children (in the abstract) were still not on my radar, I began to want my husband's children. I loved him, so I wanted us to be a family. When we left Washington, DC, I was hoping to be pregnant soon. For me, it just didn't happen in a planned time. We had a five-year wait.

In the early 1960s, my husband was called into the doctor draft, and we were stationed at an Air Force base in Michigan. It was while we were there that Betty Friedan's book *The Feminine Mystique*[2] happened. I use the word "happened," because it caused quite a stir. All the young officers' wives were reading it and talking about it. In one conversation, a friend said to me, "Oh, Ester, this doesn't apply to you." Ever since I have wished I had asked her why not, but at the time, I was silent. It did not lessen my interest in the subject, but it did tend to make it academic and unemotional. After all, I had not experienced discrimination in the workplace. If others did, well, then I was interested in the issue, but not personally involved at all.

At that time, my sister-in-law, Doris, was a graduate student at Radcliffe/Harvard, a hotbed for "women's liberation," and she and I exchanged many letters about it. Although *she* was somewhat caught up in the movement, I was still interested only intellectually.

In 1972, congress passed the Equal Rights Amendment, and it was quickly ratified by thirty-five states. It needed thirty-eight. Because I had been so involved on Capitol Hill as a young woman, and because I was familiar with the legislative process, my stake president asked me to research the legislative history of the amendment and to give firesides on the issue. The Church opposed the amendment. So did I. The fight had been to keep it broad. As I saw it, the legislators wanted to foster sameness instead of equality. I feared it would rob women of more rights than it would give them. I found it fascinating but still academic.

Along about 1977 or 78 (forty years ago, as I now write), I changed. I suppose it was because of the intensity of my witness of the reality of the gospel. In any event, my interest was no longer academic. I had begun to search the scriptures for an antidote to what I saw as the feminist invitation to misery. The antidote was there all right.[3] It was the Lord's prayer

---

2. Betty Friedan, *The Feminine Mystique* (Salt Lake City: W. W. Norton, 1963).

3. John 17:11, 22. "That they may be one, as we are."

for our oneness. I wrote a book I called *Man and Woman, Joy in Oneness.*[4] It was published by Deseret Book.

Recently I reread that book for the first time in a long time. Mostly it was because I have had occasion to have my attention directed to the world's changes in the past forty years. I think there are few changes in "the movement" for what was at first called "Women's Liberation." It was thought then that women staying in the home as wives and mothers were oppressed. Women were to be liberated from that victimization. You never hear the words "women's lib" anymore, but that is still the core of the "women's movement." The only change that has happened among women is that oppressed feelings of victimization have deepened, and certainly broadened. That is not to say there are no other changes *because of the movement.* The changes are in the world. Women's feminist desires broadened in both philosophy and with converts. Despite changes in nomenclature, the goals are unchanged, as is the antidote.

Men do have a role to play in what has happened in the world. This book is not just about women. Men and women have engaged, and do engage, in anti-oneness behaviors, and we will examine them here. There is no gender specificity in creating barriers to oneness.

We have been given divine reassurance that love and faith will make it possible to achieve the joy in oneness—and oneness is the relief of lonely frustration.

In writing this book, I have made every effort to be in harmony with scripture and modern prophets. Even so, I have felt keenly my desire to avoid being what President Dallin H. Oaks called "the instrument of pain."[5] I want to share my testimony for the single reason that I want to help men and women understand *that* they are choosing and *what* they are choosing. Sometimes, for those who have not before considered their roles from this perspective, I suppose there could be pain. If that happens, please forgive me. Always, I want to give the comfort that truth and agency can provide.

---

4. Ester Rasband, *Man and Woman, Joy in Oneness* (Salt Lake City: Deseret Book, 1982).
5. Dallin H. Oaks, *The Lord's Way* (Salt Lake City: Desert Book, 1991), 194.

PART 1

THE REASON I'M HERE: TO CHOOSE

We did not come here to obey, but to *choose* to obey.

"Our Heavenly Father's goal in parenting is not to have His children *do* what is right; it is to have His children *choose* to do what is right and ultimately become like Him. If He simply wanted us to be obedient, He would use immediate rewards and punishments to influence our behaviors."

—Dale G. Renlund
"Choose You This Day"
Ensign, Nov. 2018

CHAPTER 1

THE ATTRIBUTES
OF GODLINESS

*M*y husband and I raised our family on the Monterey Peninsula of California. Although neither of us is a golfer, to say that golf was a part of our culture would be an understatement. It seemed like the major tournaments came around more often than I am sure they did. Usually, the pros that were members of the Church gave firesides on Sunday nights. I remember one of them being particularly generous with his time and testimony. His text was always the same. He loved the gospel because it answered the three big questions: Where did I come from? Why am I here? Where am I going?

Hundreds of volumes have been written in an effort to answer each one of these questions, but I'm going to answer them in one sentence each for our purposes here and let the rest of the book, which deals mostly with question two, speak to the amplification.

Question one: Where did I come from?
Answer: From life as a spirit with my Father in Heaven.[6]

Question two: Why am I here?
Answer: To choose whether to seek for eternal life.[7]

---

6. Jeremiah 1:5.
7. Abraham 3:25.

Question three: Where am I going?

Answer: Almost certainly to a kingdom of glory.[8]

When you get right down to it, the answer to question two is by far the most important of the answers. It is a true "need to know." We need to know that we are choosing and we need to see and understand the clarity of choice. Why choice is important can be answered by answering question three: where am I going? Which kingdom and how much glory? The requirements that govern which kingdom and how much glory are not ours to modify, but which requirements to meet is a choice wide open to us. It's actually so open that we might miss knowing how to make it. It's not easy. Not easy maybe, but absolutely necessary. As Lehi and Alma told their sons, the choice is really between happiness and misery.[9] Man is that he might have joy all right, but only if he chooses it. And here's the catch: If we are a few degrees off in our focus, we could make our choices at the wrong time and in the wrong way.

One thing our Father in Heaven made clear was that it would be necessary for us to come to a fallen world where enticements of options would make it a true choice. As Lehi explained, the choice requires an environment of opposition.[10] The long-suffering and patience necessary to get through this fallen world create what seems to us a paradox. It's counterintuitive sometimes that the big choice must be made in little choices of sacrifice. Sometimes the choices are so small we hardly know we're making them. Sometimes even larger choices seem like they ought to be made for the comfort of our natural man. That's what will make us happy, right? That's what God wants for us, right? But the whole point of choosing is to put eternity first, with the willingness to sacrifice those things that stand in the way of godly development. Fortunately, though, we are given both instruction and reassurance in the scriptures. We are plainly told what can make us godly and what won't.[11]

At some point in my life (I wish I could remember when), I noticed that the scriptures were a constant repetition of what I came to call "the list." It's not a checklist, because none of its elements can ever be checked off as "done." Living it is, in fact, the most infinite of challenges. But

---

8. D&C 76.

9. 2 Nephi 2:10; Alma 40:15; Alma 41:10.

10. 2 Nephi 2:15.

11. Mosiah 3:19; 2 Peter 1.

make no mistake. It helps[12] in recognizing and knowing how to make the choices, little or big, if you want to grow to godliness. It can get us through the opposition—both of our own making and the painful problems offered by the fallen world. That is because it tells us the governing principles for what sacrifices will have to be made.[13]

As I repeatedly found the list, I started noticing things about it. Some scriptural writers talked of only a few of the virtues on it, and some were very complete indeed. That which I call the list is frequently labeled as "charity." President Dallin H. Oaks, probably following the lead of the Prophet Joseph Smith, called it "the principles of righteousness."[14] The summary for section 4 of the Doctrine and Covenants sets forth what I call the "attributes of godliness" list. I do love that name for the list, because calling it (truthfully) "the attributes of godliness" explains why those attributes are so hard to live.

Perhaps my favorite place to find the list is where it is most poetic. It is in 1 Corinthians 13:1–7. Apparently, the Saints in Corinth had the same sort of predispositions we have.

> 1 Though I speak with the tongues of men and of angels, and have not charity, I am become as sounding brass, or a tinkling cymbal.
>
> 2 And though I have the gift of prophecy, and understand all mysteries, and all knowledge; and though I have all faith, so that I could remove mountains, and have not charity, I am nothing.
>
> 3 And though I bestow all my goods to feed the poor, and though I give my body to be burned, and have not charity, it profiteth me nothing.
>
> 4 Charity suffereth long, and is kind; charity envieth not; charity vaunteth not itself, is not puffed up,
>
> 5 Doth not behave itself unseemly, seeketh not her own, is not easily provoked, thinketh no evil;
>
> 6 Rejoiceth not in iniquity, but rejoiceth in the truth;
>
> 7 Beareth all things, believeth all things, hopeth all things, endureth all things.

---

12. 2 Peter 1:9.
13. 1 Corinthians 13:11.
14. Ibid.; Oaks, *The Lord's Way*, 206; D&C 121:45.

I also like what seems to be the most complete list in Doctrine and Covenants 107:30–31. Here it is given to the First Presidency and the Quorum of the Twelve who will be required to speak for the Lord and make decisions in His Holy Name:

30 The decisions of these quorums, or either of them, are to be made in all righteousness, in holiness, and lowliness of heart, meekness and long-suffering, and in faith, and virtue, and knowledge, temperance, patience, godliness, brotherly kindness and charity;

31 Because the promise is, if these things abound in them they shall not be unfruitful in the knowledge of the Lord.

The promise that we will not be unfruitful in our knowledge implies a harvest. The concept of "harvest," in turn, implies plowing and planting. We search the scriptures for the intent of following. There we find the attributes of godliness—the very definition of love—the all-important list of the principles of righteousness. Then, if that uncheckoffable list governs our heart and mind, we will understand God and His ways.[15] That is the promised harvest. That understanding witness—that knowing—will be the fruit of our labors in the list. We will be reaching toward the ultimate charity: the great, free gift of eternal life that is ours to choose. Without the list as our focus, neither the law nor the prophets[16] will open the beauty of their meaning to us.[17] But when that beauty, that knowledge of joy is opened, we choose to make those every day choices to sacrifice whatever is necessary to make the big choice for eternal joy.[18]

When the choice is made, we understand why we are nothing[19] without what the scriptures sometimes call charity, sometimes call joy, and most often call love. It is the pure white fruit,[20] a gift from God, freely given if we but choose it. Choose it behaviorally.[21]

The scriptures define eternal life as knowing God the Eternal Father and Jesus Christ whom He hast sent.[22] So the choice of question two is

---

15. 2 Peter 1:8.
16. See Luke 10.
17. 2 Peter 1:9.
18. Joshua 24:15.
19. Mosiah 4:5; Moses 1:10.
20. 1 Nephi 15:36.
21. James 14:20.
22. John 17:3.

the choice to try to know Christ—or not. According to Peter,[23] Joseph Smith,[24] Lehi,[25] Alma,[26] Moses,[27] and, in fact, many modern prophets, it is our desire to have the attributes of godliness that will determine that knowledge of Christ. Or, in other words, how we have made the choice that is the purpose of this life.[28]

Joseph Smith said that it is necessary to have a correct idea of the character of God before eternal life becomes possible.[29] If we don't understand godly attributes, it's easy to make mistakes about what is right in their eyes and what is not. Obedience is, of course, the primary evidence of our desire to live again with God, who cannot look at sin with the least degree of allowance.[30] We are not being honest with ourselves if we think we want to live again with God but don't want to live in His way. So what all of this means is that seeking eternal life is to reach toward knowledge of Christ, which is also seeking knowledge of God the Father. (They are one in character after all.)[31] The knowledge necessary to make the choice requires a desire to know the law for the purpose of knowing Christ. The law is a means, not an end.[32]

Therefore, if we are to choose to seek eternal life, we must follow the advice of the Prophet Joseph Smith[33] and correctly understand godly character for the purpose of working toward ultimately having that same character ourselves.[34] Because that's what eternal life is. It is to be given a perfection of love, charity, and pure white fruit forever. And that is what we came here to decide: Do we want it or not?

The character of Christ is not easy to develop. Maybe we'll want to choose otherwise. Christ's character, after all, led Him to be crucified

---

23. Ibid.; 2 Peter 1:8.
24. *Lectures on Faith* (1985), 3.
25. 2 Nephi 2:16.
26. Alma 38:2–3.
27. Moses 1:20.
28. 2 Chronicles 15:15. ("And all Judah rejoiced at the oath: for they had sworn with all their heart, and sought him with their whole desire; and he was found of them: and the LORD gave them rest round about.")
29. Ibid., *Lectures on Faith.*
30. Alma 45:16.
31. John 10:30.
32. 2 Chronicles 25:2.
33. Ibid.
34. 3 Nephi 27:27.

for sins that others committed. And He did it because it was the will of His Father[35] and His own divine loving desire as well.[36] WOW! No wonder the path is narrow, and no wonder few there be that find it.[37] We came here to an opposition-filled, fallen world to have the opportunity to prove that we want to be like Him. Unlike Christ, we can't atone for the sins of others, but we can show our trust that Christ will do it and work at loving our enemies.[38] Unlike Christ, we cannot be perfect in mortality, but we can, through submission to Him, make ourselves perfectible by Him.[39] That's the possibility for us. He only awaits our firm decision to choose Him.

A variety of decisions happen on our way through a fallen world. Many of them can stand as barriers to knowing and emulating the character of Christ and our Father in Heaven. Our inadequate knowledge doesn't always see our choices for what they are. Remember it is rarely one big choice but a series of little ones that show our preference. Our small decisions to act can still constitute a negative choice whether we think so or not.[40]

Change of path can happen to anyone along the way. Even people whose early choices are for a celestial goal do sometimes change. Those seekers can end up not enduring. Enduring in love, it turns out, is a sizable challenge. In the face of opposition, it can be so much more pleasing to seek one's own. It's not unusual to choose to turn away from following the simple, but sacrificing, method of gaining godly knowledge. At every stage of life, enticements come. Fortunately, just as we can change to leave the path, we can change to get onto it.[41] The gracious Atonement of Christ is the enabling ordinance.

Many dip their toe into the lake of knowledge (myself among them). They may even wade a bit. No mortal can swim in it eternally without the perfection offered by Christ through His Atonement. What we are free to choose is whether or not to become perfectible by going deeper and deeper into the living water of love.[42] More often than not, I fear,

---

35. John 6:38.
36. D&C 4:3.
37. Matthew 7:14.
38. 3 Nephi 12.
39. Moroni 10:32; D&C 88:29–31.
40. Alma 37:6.
41. Alma 5:7.
42. John 7:38.

if we stay in the shallow water, some choice comes along that makes us at least consider turning back to seek the dry land of worldly self-fulfillment. We stay in the shallow water when we live the gospel as a checklist instead of the love list. We stay in the shallow water whenever we focus on a sense of entitlement instead of on sharing the Lord's mission of sacrifice. At some point in the shallow water, we shiver with cold, because only by going into the deeper water of love is there warmth. Standing there shivering, the self-focused comfort of dry land is indeed tempting, even if we know it is not eternal. That may be what we want to choose. We came here to make that decision.

Going to church, having the fellowship of the Saints, and daily scripture reading will help in the decision process, but those righteous activities are not the big decision itself. The choice is made by the aggregate of our behavior that shows reaching to fulfill our roles to love in the Lord's way and on the Lord's mission.[43] It's a matter of what comes first to us, a matter of trusting the Lord, who gives us our roles in the plan of salvation. Trusting with fulness of heart or not. Only love and desire will lead us to obedient discipleship.[44]

We don't have Christ's role. There is only one "Only Begotten." But we do have a role, a sacrificing role. If we want it, it will be revealed to us. Almost always the revelation will come through scriptures and/or modern prophets.[45] Always it will require our working at the godly attributes that are the character of Christ, and always it will include our being willing to do it because it is the will of our Father and our own loving desire. It was true for Christ and it must be true for us. Perhaps one of the important things we must remember here on earth is this: Our role is not to *play* God but to *obey* God. That obedience defines love. Only in that love can we hope to *know* God. And true depth of obedience comes from understanding the godly attributes. Our faith is as fragile as our understanding.

We may not think of our wanting things our way as playing God, but if we think we know better what is best for us than He does, well, it's a kind of replacing His knowledge with our own, ergo, so many passages of scripture warning us about trusting in the arm of flesh.[46]

---

43. John 21:16–17.
44. John 14:15.
45. Russell M. Nelson, "Opening Remarks," *Ensign*, Nov. 2018.
46. 2 Nephi 4:34.

One of our problems of trust shows itself in wanting our own definitions of godly language. We are willing to accept that love is the core, all right, but we have a very different definition for love. We want God's love for us to be a denial of our sins instead of a deep sorrow about them. We want Him to "love me for what I am" instead of loving us enough to help us be something more. We want to declare what God's love is instead of seeing the reality of it. We want to love a permissive God instead of a lifting one. We need to share the conviction of Enos and the brother of Jared, that He is "a God of truth and canst not lie,"[47] so we accept His definition of love instead of clinging to our own. Wanting it, choosing it, and sacrificing for it will not only enable us to know Christ ourselves but will make it easier for others to gain that desire and make that choice. It is therefore, our part of the plan of salvation to exercise these attributes in the roles the Lord provides for us. It is the yoke that He sweetly made possible for us to share with Him.[48] We can actually participate in both the giving and receiving of the plan. Isn't that amazing? And perhaps the most amazing part of all is the seeming paradox of peace that will come into our lives when we cease seeking our own.[49]

Our desire for a permissive God instead of one whose wisdom knows better what our joy can be has led us to a place where, as Isaiah described it, we call evil good and good evil.[50] I'm reminded of a joke that made the rounds when it was still considered ridiculous. A "hippie" saw a man lying in the street, the victim of a hit and run driver. He approached the man with his version of love: "I love you, man," he said. The man struggled out the words, "Call me an ambulance." The hippie responded, "Sure, man. You're an ambulance!" That joke would probably be politically incorrect today, but in terms of thinking that we can declare what love really is, it's still funny. God's love is not permissive, but with repentance, it is forgiving. God's love is not ours to define, but it is ours to reach toward.

In a Gospel Doctrine class a few years ago, we were studying Lehi's vision of the tree of life. Our wise instructor said this: "The iron rod is the word of God. *The* word of God is love." Later, in my individual study,

---

47. Ether 3:12; Enos 1:6.
48. Matthew 11:29.
49. 1 Corinthians 13:5.
50. Isaiah 5:20–21.

I came to a deeper understanding of that truth. For me, now, the vision uses three different symbols of love: the iron rod, the fruit of the tree of life, and the river of water. The iron rod is the love that manifests as His word to us. This includes the commandments and covenants. The Tree of (eternal) Life yields pure, delicious, perfect love, which we can be eternally given.

The third symbol, I believe, is of the dangerous polluted love of the worldly definition. Frequently in the scriptures, I see water as a symbol of love. Love, like water, after all, is life sustaining and cleansing. I believe that the filthy river of water[51] is the perverted pollution of love that is the worldly definition of it. Filthy water is no longer cleansing and ironically can be the poison that takes life. Hanging on to the loving word of God, that is to say obeying the commandments and keeping our covenants, will stop us from falling into the worldly self-indulgent version of love. Hanging on requires focused, consecrated hearts. When Nephi was treated to an interpretation of his father's vision, it revealed to him something about his father: "So much was his mind swallowed up in other things that he beheld not the filthiness of the water."[52] Like Lehi, we can be oblivious to the worldliness going on around us. The goal of tasting the pure, white fruit will absolutely possess and direct us.

Those of us who are given the most ideal opportunities to practice God's definition of love and therefore to know Christ (that is to say, the ideal of having the opportunities to teach a family how to love) must give those teaching and loving roles grateful focus by the effort to live the attributes of godliness. It must be something we seize with all of our desire. Those roles, those ideal opportunities are outlined for us in the family proclamation.[53] We need to deeply desire those opportunities to reach toward a perfectible portion of the pure love of Christ in our lives. And when we are not given here the ideal, we must still govern our lives with the list. It's harder without the ideal, but it can yield the same knowledge, that is to say, the knowledge of Christ—the fount of all knowledge—and the atoning conduit to the perfect love of our Father in Heaven.

---

51. 1 Nephi 15:25–28.
52. 1 Nephi 15:27.
53. "The Family: A Proclamation to the World" (Salt Lake City: The Church of Jesus Christ of Latter-day Saints, 1995), *Ensign* or *Liahona*, Nov. 2010, 129.

It is no accident that long-suffering and patience are part of the list. They will be required—as will leaving off seeking our own and vaunting ourselves. They are part of the submission about which King Benjamin speaks,[54] the sacrifice that choosing to know Christ will call on us to make. As the favorite hymn[55] reminds us: they are the sacrifices that will bring forth the blessings of Heaven. They are what we must choose . . . or not choose as our resolution of the answer to that all-important middle question: "Why am I here?

> For they being ignorant of God's righteousness, and going about to establish their own righteousness, have not submitted themselves unto the righteousness of God.[56]

And last, but not less important to the exercise of faith in God, is the idea that He is love. All the other excellencies in His character, without this one to influence them, couldn't have such powerful dominion over the minds of men. But when the idea is planted in the mind that He is love, who cannot see the just ground that men of every nation, kindred, and tongue have to exercise faith in God so as to obtain eternal life?

---

54. Mosiah 3:19.
55. "Praise to the Man," *Hymns*, no. 27, verse 4.
56. Romans 10:3.

CHAPTER 2

NURTURING

*A*ccording to "The Family: A Proclamation to the World," in the most godly situations, a woman's mission is full-time nurturing. The hymn "Sisters in Zion"[57] calls woman's role the "errand of angels." That is certainly what it feels like.

Our mission is not an easy one. At its best, nurturing is completely self-sacrificing. At its worst, it is grudging and resentful. The truth is that grudging resentment ends up not being nurturing at all.

The mission to nurture is given in the most general of terms, but it requires the most specific of actions. The creativity and ingenuity required are greater than for any other activity. It is the work of God himself.[58] I have a young friend in her early forties who is particularly good at this, and I'd like to use her as a definer of what I am describing. She is a superb detective. She looks into the souls of others and knows what their wants and needs are. She has full-time employment (I should mention that she is single), so her nurturing time is limited, but it is intensely tailored to the individuals she serves. As one of them, I can tell you that she hits it on the head every time. She gives me exactly what I want and need, and gives it with such a lack of expectation that it amazes me.

I happen to know that she also cares deeply about others and serves them all differently. It's rarely about what she wants to give, but mostly about what is needed or wanted by those she serves. She goes to bed dead tired every night, because we who are nurtured by her have used her up.

---

57. "As Sisters in Zion," *Hymns*, no. 309, verse 2.
58. Ezra Taft Benson, "A Star of the First Magnitude," *Ensign*, Dec. 1985.

Her professional demands are great as well and often require uneven hours. I suspect that when she is old she will be able to say, with President Spencer W. Kimball, that she is a worn out pair of old shoes in the Lord's service.[59] And the Lord will welcome her into His arms.

While we are talking of singles, I want to mention a distant relative that I've never met. Her name was Mima, and she lived into her nineties. It doesn't seem to matter where I go, people still ask me if I am related to Mima. She taught first grade in Provo and was a great nurturer of her students, as well as all the people in her neighborhood. There are so many stories about people Mima cared for! She made a difference in her world.

Actually, singles (like the two I've talked about) make a choice to nurture that is not forced upon them. They accept the errand of angels of their own free will and choice. Married people can feel compelled to serve, because we are surrounded by those who need us every moment of every day. Married mothers are often the ones who feel grudging and resentful. By the Lord's definition, it seems like that isn't nurturing at all. Feeling that one is "required" to do something can do that. But if that feeling attends our nurturing, then it is without the Lord's self-losing definition of love, and therefore probably does not truly nurture.

His definition is to further His mission on earth by caring for His other children. I love to watch true nurturers—both single and married—in their creative and ingenious labors of love.

Francis Bacon, the seventeenth century philosopher, was once asked why he had never married. He replied that it would have been hard to do the mission he chose of "watering the world" if he had a well to fill at home.[60] He, of course, did not have the restored gospel and did not know that the well to fill at home was as important as it is. He was without knowledge of the eternal role of the family unit. Nevertheless, he clearly knew through the light of Christ that we are here to—one way or another—give nurturing nourishment to our fellows. It is most important to fill the wells we have at home, but when those roles are not in our lives, we are still on the Lord's mission and therefore are preparing to meet God when we water the world.

---

59. Quoted by Boyd K. Packer in "The Twelve," *Ensign*, May 2008. ("My life is like my shoes—to be worn out in service.")
60. Rasband, *Man and Woman, Joy in Oneness*, 46.

The young woman I spoke of before tells me that early on in her adult life she was taught that whether she married or not, the best way to prepare for eternal motherhood was to make the goals of others her own goals. She tells me now that the rewards have not been just the preparation for another life. She receives rich dividends of love from those who have been the recipient of hers. And the numbers are staggering.

Once long ago, I received a little framed proverb as a gift. It said, "I am the place God's love shines through." With the passing of years, I've misplaced it. Perhaps I should have a new one made so I can give one to my young friend.

It's true, you know. As Christ told us and as King Benjamin foretold, when we are in the service of our fellow man we are only in the service of our God.[61] When we nurture one another, we are not just on the errand of angels. We are on the errand of our Heavenly Father himself.[62]

Women who are mothers have a unique opportunity to embrace and magnify the role of nurturer. It is an incredibly important opportunity.

Whoever does the nurturing is the one who has the most power in the lives of others. The reason is that they have more influence than any other role affords. Funny isn't it, that so many see control as power, when the greatest power is that which lasts beyond the time of control. It is *influence* that lasts in minds and hearts now and forever.[63] To think that some sacrifice that opportunity to have lasting power for some short-term feeling of being in charge—well, it saddens me.

And the paradox happens. But then, we have come to expect that, haven't we? Everybody fights to sit by my young friend who always seeks those who need her. And everybody wants to know if I'm related to Mima so that they can praise her to me. Praise her to the skies!

It's truly Christlike to be identified as He was: "We love Him, because He first loved us."[64]

Still, people guard against giving too much. They fear that their self will disappear. This fear particularly raises its ugly head in marriage. It is now widely taught that a marriage is the uniting of two people

---

61. Matthew 25:40; Mosiah 2:17.
62. Mosiah 2:17.
63. D&C 121:45.
64. 1 John 4:19.

who will stay individuals—a far cry from the cleaving to and "owning" one another that Paul said must be.[65] It certainly is in contradiction of becoming one flesh.[66]

It is a philosophy of *men* that we should be so careful about losing ourselves. God said, "seek ye first the kingdom of God, and his righteousness"[67] if we want all else to be added unto us. The kingdom and its righteousness are, of course, summarized by the two great commandments: Love God and love one another.[68] Love can be defined as what we feel when we care enough for others that we want to sacrifice for them. Only love enables us to know Christ.[69]

While the scriptures teach to find the kingdom of God first, the world has a contrasting corollary. The world says to find yourself and all else will be added unto you. God says lose yourself for His sake and you will find yourself.[70] "For His sake" is an interesting and meaningful phrase. He has already defined love of your neighbor as "like unto it." He has already both hinted and clearly stated that doing acts of love and sacrifice for others is the same as doing it unto Him. That is because it is "for His sake" to participate in His mission of bringing to pass the eternal life of others.[71]

Guarding of the self is a contradiction to nurturing. Those who believe that the best relationships are between "individuals" who carefully do not sacrifice their individuality will never be able to nurture in the Lord's way. God does and will always value us as "individuals." But, for us, we must value our ability to be one with others. That is His instruction.[72] That is what God expects of those who love Him with their heart, might, mind, and strength. That means nurturing others, holding nothing back. "Heart, might, mind, and strength" is another way of saying

---

65. 1 Corinthians 7:4.
66. Genesis 2:24: "Therefore shall a man leave his father and his mother, and shall cleave unto his wife: and they shall be one flesh." Mark 10:8: "And they twain shall be one flesh: so then they are no more twain, but one flesh."
67. Matthew 6:33.
68. Matthew 6:36–40.
69. 2 Peter 1:9; 2 Nephi 26:30.
70. Matthew 16:25.
71. Moses 1:39; Matthew 11:29.
72. John 17:21.

we must consecrate ourselves to His mission. No guarding ourselves, no holding back.

If we choose to nurture, we are, after all, doing it in His name and for His sake.

I was once in a class where the teacher said that God has a special place for individuals. He calls it outer darkness. I think that may be a bit extreme. Many of the worst of us self-seekers will have a chance to repent after the millennium.[73] But I do believe that the opposite is surely true: God has a special place for list-living, self-sacrificing, nurturers. It is a place of bright and eternal light. He calls it exaltation.

> Wherefore, the Lord God hath given a commandment that all men should have charity, which charity is love. And except they should have charity they were nothing.[74]

> Great shall be their reward and eternal life shall be their glory.[75]

---

73. See D&C 76:109.
74. 2 Nephi 26:30.
75. D&C 76:6.

Chapter 3

Destination Orientation

On an airplane going to Tasmania from mainland Australia, I sat next to a young Tasmanian man who had just spent a week with a young woman in Sydney. He was obviously consumedly smitten. He was eager to talk about her and the passionate week he had just spent. He extolled the girl's beauty, her intellect, and her kindness. After a while, I asked him whether and when there were marriage plans.

"Oh, we don't think about destinations," he said. It's all about the journey. The wonderful journey!" Then he got a little melancholy. "I do realize that it won't last. These things never do."

"What things?" I asked. "Are you talking about your young woman's beauty and intellect and kindness?"

"No," he said, "of course not. I'm sure I'll always see those things in her. I'll probably always have tender feelings for her. But appreciation isn't being in love, and I don't want to think about the end of the thrill. I don't believe in thinking about the end of anything. I like to concentrate on the journey. Nothing else. Just the journey."

He returned to talking about the passion of the week and the "incredible journey."

I only half listened then, but he went on and on about his week of destination-free gratification for his all-consuming physical ache. His journey orientation was not open to deeper and higher thought. At that moment, he could not have understood that his focus on the temporary was part of a choosing process for which he had come into this world. He didn't want to think about the end of anything, but mortality does have an end. Unless we use this temporary life to focus on a destination where we can no longer have to worry about good things not lasting, our fears will cloud our journey.

I wanted to tell him about destination-oriented relationships and how that which cannot remain a constant can evolve into something that is much better defined as love than what he was experiencing now. I wanted to tell him about the list. I wanted to tell him about the love that comes out of the spirit—the love that focuses on the Lord, your partner, their goals, and the family you can become. I wanted to tell him how that becomes a passion in itself. I wanted to tell him that even the physical ache for one another can be more delightfully deepened by having a purposeful destination of endlessness together. Instead of temporary unbridled passion, I wanted him to have a critical mass of love. I wanted him to have the amazing knowledge that he could have a role in the plan of salvation.

What an irony of life it is that only with a focus on destination does the journey itself acquire meaning and richness. As I sat on the airplane that day, it became a symbol of mortality to me. I conjured up visions of sitting there in that uncomfortable seat, not knowing that where I was going would be worth it—thinking only about the trip itself and not about the beauty of the destination. How weary one would get of the trip. I thought of how important anticipation is to delight in the trip. My young traveling companion doesn't want to think of endings because he fears them. Only perfect love casts out fear. Temporary passion certainly cannot. No wonder "these things never last." I thought of my own marriage, how my goals and my husband's goals had so naturally evolved into family goals because the beauty of our destination had over committed time become so clear to us. If only we could have a world full of people committed to the family proclamation.

Afterward I thought about the journey-focused marriages I knew and how sad I found them. Then I thought of the marriages I knew where only one spouse was focused on the eternal destination. I pitied them about as much. But maybe not quite as much after all. The situation is not so hopeless. As Paul pointed out, it's possible for the righteous spouse to sanctify the other.[76] In any case, I would so much rather be the

---

76. 1 Corinthians 7:14.

spouse that put the destination first. Even alone that is the happier role. I suppose that is because of the partnership in the plan of salvation that we can feel even just between ourselves and God. It is in that unity with our Father in Heaven that we find our peace—both in the journey and the destination.

When I got engaged, I received a letter from my brother. Marriage, he told me, is all about giving. Divorce, he said, is all about thinking you are giving too much. "When you are having those divorce-type feelings, the antidote is not to give less, but to give more. Giving has power. And rest assured, your Father in Heaven is watching you. If you don't show Him you like being a wife, He will not trouble you with that role in the eternities." I think my brother was telling me to keep my eye on the destination.

Giving, including forgiving, requires the destination orientation. That means wanting to reach toward the perfection that only Christ's Atonement can offer. Trying to love the Lord's way for the Lord's purposes will never mean capitulating to unrighteousness. We must give long-suffering and patience, but not indulgence. We get back to accepting the Lord's definitions instead of insisting on our own. Our natural man can believe that giving means giving in to a unity with sin. But the Lord's definition is in "the list." It means to "seek not our own." It means to seek the strength through our faith to love someone who is behaving like our enemy—to lose ourselves for the Lord's sake. That means to always remember that we came here to choose whether to seek a Christlike eternity by intensely desiring to take on what we can of Christ's mission here. That mission is to love and forgive to make it easier for someone we love to do his own reaching. No one can tell another what the Lord's definition of giving will be in an individual situation (what will make it easier and what will make it harder). Only the spirit can direct that, but one thing is certain, "giving" will never include seeking your own or trying to receive that spiritual guidance without putting your efforts into loving others in the first place.

That is what a destination orientation really means, and it is the only way to know Christ.

That letter from my brother was a heavy dose of hard doctrine, but I have come to know that it is true doctrine. Resentment of giving is a journey orientation. To focus on journey is a focus on what Elder Maxwell reminded us has a short shelf life.[77]

The eternal destination of becoming part of the family of Christ, with all the responsibility and reward of perfect love that eternity brings with it, will also bring bumps in the road of our mortal journey. I can't repeat often enough that long-suffering and patience are high on "the list." They have to be. The question we came to earth to answer is this: are they *worth it* to us? If they are not, we will turn away from the sacrifices involved in the giving that my brother talked of. When we step back from that requirement, it won't improve the journey. On the contrary, the journey will be only fleetingly "thrilling" or, at worst, lastingly resentful. The destination will be obscured to our vision in any case.[78]

Experience teaches us that troubled time is a particularly important choosing time. The key is to get beyond feeling deprived and taken advantage of. To feel loved and valued, we must focus on the destination of becoming exalted. If we do that, no matter how bumpy the road, we will be happier. Love that does that.

What makes the journey both joyful and subordinate is that, as Amulek said, "This life is the time to prepare to meet God."[79] And as Lehi said, God will consecrate our affliction for our gain.[80] As President Nelson said, "For Latter-day Saints, Jesus Christ is joy!"[81]

President Hinckley used to tell us that we need to have fun and laughter along the way. I deeply believe that. It's just the paradox: fun, laughter, and the light heart are, ironically, byproducts of focusing on our eternal destination. I think that is because the change of focus eliminates the fear of good things ending. When we know what we are choosing, we know that the negatives are temporary, not the positives. As the young man on the airplane suggested, he was acutely aware of the temporary nature of his "thrill." Wouldn't it be so much better to have a conviction of its permanence instead? Focus on the requirements for our

---

77. Neal A. Maxwell, "The Tugs and Pulls of the World," *Ensign*, Nov. 2000. "We are free to choose the mortal perks with their short shelf life. However, ahead lies that great moment when every knee shall bow and every tongue confess that Jesus is the Christ!" (See Mosiah 27:31 and D&C 88:104.)
78. Ibid.; see 2 Peter.
79. Alma 34:32.
80. 2 Nephi 2:2.
81. "Joy and Spiritual Survival," *Ensign*, Nov. 2016.

eternal destination is necessary to reach a critical mass of love that the young man on the plane didn't understand, so he feared the ending of "the thrill." The primary requirement is the giving my brother told me to commit to.

Just as physicists learned that certain minimums of material were necessary before a chain reaction of nuclear energy started to happen, we must understand that certain minimums of desire, choice, and sacrifice must accumulate in our hearts to create a climate of perfectibility. Christ can give new birth to our hearts only when they are broken. Our Savior can enlarge our spirits only when they are contrite. The "mighty change"[82] we read about in the scriptures describes that point in our progress when the minimums are reached and a mighty eternal chain reaction of perfectibility is begun in our souls. The physicists call the minimum of material a "critical mass." That which I have called a critical mass of love in man is a minimum of the love of God—enough love of God the Father and His son Jesus Christ to cause desire to sacrifice to know Him.

It is a glorious plan. Even the minimums that constitute a critical mass for the Lord to work on, will introduce us to our potential. I love the way President Monson talks of the process.

"God left the world unfinished for man to work his skill upon. He left the electricity in the cloud, the oil in the earth. He left the rivers unbridged and the forests unfelled and the cities unbuilt. God gives to man the challenge of raw materials, not the ease of finished things. He leaves the pictures unpainted, the music unsung, and the problems unresolved, that man may know the joys and glories of creation."[83]

As Peter said, it is through the great and precious promises that we can become partakers of the divine nature.[84] Or, in other words, start the chain reaction of perfectibility. If our consecrating covenants to give are kept, the Spirit will visit us with an intensity of the feelings of the list for God and for others. It's a critical mass of love. The most "worth it" wants in our lives will always be for the good of the unit that man and woman and their family have become. And the ultimate good for them all will be eternal life. If that is our choice, each will serve that destination, whether our actions are on our own or in concert with a spouse. Salvation, after

---

82. Mosiah 5:2.
83. Thomas S. Monson, "In Quest of the Abundant Life," *Ensign*, Mar. 1988.
84. 2 Peter 1:2.

all, is individual. It is that individual salvation that makes us eligible to be part of an exalted family.

In our journey-obsessed world, roles in families are seen as limiting. We need to be far more trusting in the Lord's wisdom. In mortality, the roles we take will be sometimes on the center stage. Sometimes they will be support roles. The support role is what we take for the good of the partnership and therefore it is for our own benefit as certainly as the center stage role.

There are recognizable signs that we are focusing on "the journey" instead of the destination. One of them is talk of "your turn" and "my turn." Turns do indeed take place in who has the support role and who has the center stage, but those turns evolve in a relationship where the best interest of the eternal partnership is what is sought. When you have a destination that comes first in your mind, you are not focused on whose turn it is to shine. You are both serving the desired result. Turns in the spotlight change naturally when oneness is present. They may change minute to minute, year to year, or even decade to decade. To a destination-focused couple, it doesn't matter. Both are benefitting and both serving. Turns are given by circumstance, not taken or coveted by a mortal journey focus.

Commitment to the best eternal destination, with an eye to making it easier for our spouses to share the goal, is a good example of list-living love. I think that our choice to commit to loving will make us, line upon line, able to abide a forever of perfect love. And that is the destination toward which we must stay oriented if our choices are to lead us to reach a critical mass of love. At that point, the decision for which we came to this earth will have been made. Our "portion"[85] will be perfectible, and His grace will be sufficient for us.[86]

Seek ye first the kingdom of God and his righteousness and all these things shall be added unto you.[87]

---

85. D&C 88:29.
86. Moroni 10:32.
87. Matthew 6:33.

CHAPTER 4

STEWARDSHIP AND CRITICAL MASS

Several decades back, I had a dear friend whose first baby turned out to be twin girls. Most new mothers are welcoming, but she was even more so. She was amazingly joyful. There was no postpartum depression, just all the heavy, double-duty work, which she never complained about. Then, after a year or year and a half passed, she started complaining. It was more than just complaint. She snapped at her babies and her husband and was not too pleasant to be around for others either. She identified her behavior as "anger management problems," and she went to see a therapist.

After a short couple of months of therapy, she discovered something about herself. She wanted those little girls so much that the first year was all about having her hopes and dreams fulfilled. But as Jean Kerr has beautifully said, "Once you have children, you *have them*."[88] Taking care of those little girls became a requirement and not just a loving choice. It had stopped being service and become servitude. As long as it was her choice, she was happy to give. Once the care became a requirement, she felt taken advantage of, and she resented it.

The therapist's recommendation, unfortunately, was that she put the girls in day care and do what sounded delightful to her. The therapist recognized that choosing what she most wanted was crucial to her well-being. I call it "unfortunate," because if he could have instead helped

---

88. Jean Kerr, *The Snake Has All the Lines* (New York: Doubleday, 1960), preface.

her to see the eternal significance in her motherhood and the profound value of raising those babies, she just might have chosen, once again, to give herself to those little girls. Because it would have been her choice, it would have become delightful again. I'm sure it would not have removed the fatigue and frustration. Rest and respite were needed, and her denial of that need earlier probably meant she had some catch-up to do in that department. As King Benjamin told his people, "It is not necessary for man to run faster than he has strength. All things must be done in wisdom and order."[89]

As I understand the problem, though (and as pointed out by her therapist), she did not see it as a need for rest and respite—no matter how much that may have helped. She needed to see it as that simple need. She needed to continue being the one who cared for those babies. But it wasn't a matter of just seeing herself as unable to keep going without rejuvenation. That was not her complaint. For her, it had become a matter of not wanting to mother anymore. It was a matter of her feeling required to do something she wasn't choosing.

Perhaps no amount of help would have made a difference. She might still have chosen as she did. Perhaps, for some reason unknown to me, she had stopped loving, and therefore lost that sustaining power.

As was recognized by both her and her therapist, it was desire and choice that made the difference. It is, however, necessary to ask ourselves a question or two about "desire" and how it is obtained. Our desire need not mean capitulation to our natural man. We are capable of tapping into a higher level of desire. We are capable of overriding our default emotions with an eternal perspective. We are capable of judgment as to what is *worth it*.

Wouldn't it have been lovely had the therapist tried to elevate her understanding of her value to her children? Might that have made a difference in her desire?

I still remember clearly the conversation we had when she explained it all to me. I understood immediately. That was the moment I began understanding the power in choice and love. Having been the sole caregiver for twins for more than a year is something few women can do without complaint. Even though I had not yet had children, I knew that much. But for that long period, my friend was empowered by her love and her choice. A clear case of "they ain't heavy, they're my children."

---

89. See Mosiah 4:27.

The combination of love and choice turns many a human being into what some of us would call superheroes.

It turned out that her therapy was life-changing for me, as well as for my friend. I immediately recognized in my own "natural man" the same problem. Not so much about mothering, especially since I did not have children at the time, but I could see it in all kinds of my behavior. When it was my idea and on my terms, I was happy to serve others. When they started expecting it and asking me for things, I complained. I felt taken advantage of. When service was an outright assignment, when it became an absolute "stewardship," well, that was worse. I wanted to do everything "my way."

I started observing others who apparently had the same "natural man" problems that I did. It was more common than not. Also, more common than not, was to act on the problem the way the therapist had suggested: Choose the delight of your "natural man" instead of examining what has more value so that you might desire to change your choice. Making your stewardship your "own will" can change both your life and your eternity.

We often point to the fact that even if it is not our stewardship, what we are choosing to give is good. There is truth in the fact that our chosen activity may benefit others. If our "own will" serves others (laudable indeed and yielding great gratitude from those others), then we tell ourselves that our stewardship is less important than the great good we are doing—or even that these other services we have chosen to do have become our stewardship. I heard one woman say it in plain language: "I have chosen my own path to celestial life." We are, of course, free to believe whatever we like, but not to change truth. No other activity—for money or as a volunteer—can be a substitute for the stewardships that are God given.[90] The family proclamation, as well as our four volumes of scripture, speak loudly about those stewardships.

Christ was careful for us to understand that He did what He did for two reasons: the first was always that it was the will of the Father.[91] The second was that His own love for us was such that He would give His pain and His life for us.[92] When Christ was asked what manner of

---

90. "No other success can compensate for failure in the home." (David O. McKay, 136th Semiannual General Conference, September 30, 1966.)

91. 3 Nephi 27:13–14.

92. D&C3 4:3.

man the rest of us should be, He answered, "even as I am."[93] I believe
with all my heart that those motivating reasons are what He meant for
our mortal beings to do and be: that submission to His Father in Heaven
and that love for His Father and for us. That's what He wanted us to
emulate. That must be our goal. He and His prophets have taught those
perfectible principles in every possible way. If we would be "even as He
is" for eternity, that is to say exalted, celestial beings, we have to love God
enough to do *His* will, and we have to love our fellow man enough to
joyfully accept our stewardship for them.

I say that we "have to," but, of course, you know the defining part of
that statement is "if we would have exalted, celestial life." We only "have
to" if we want that. So many of us think that's what we want. I wonder
how many of us really want it or are simply involved in self-delusion.
Our Father in Heaven understands our hearts and where our true priorities lie. If perfect love is not a responsibility that appeals to us, He knows.
He's only watching our desire to see what portion we will present to
Him: celestial, terrestrial, or telestial.[94] The stewardships we accept and
the degree of humble devoted love with which we accept them will constitute whatever critical mass of love that will enable a chain reaction.[95]

We do not have the mission of Christ, and in any event cannot be
perfect enough to even compare ourselves to Him or our missions to His.
Nevertheless, we can, and must, reach toward having His motives, and
in so doing, become perfectible. That is to say: able to abide His perfect
love forever.

From His point of view, He wants us all to be with Him.[96] He loves
us. But our point of view may be different. There is only one thing He
wants more than our eternity with Him. That one thing is that we be
free to choose for ourselves.[97] That is because only in our own choices is it
possible for us to be joyful. We hope that we can learn to use that agency
to make choices of eternal love instead of the fleeting desires of our natural man. If we remember always that we are continually making choices,

---

93. 3 Nephi 27:27.
94. D&C 8:22–25.
95. D&C 8.
96. Matthew 23:37.
97. Abraham 3:25; 2 Nephi 2:26.

and if we choose to live the commandments, God the Father and His Holy Son are more likely to get what They really want—and so are we.[98]

> And all Judah rejoiced at the oath: for they had sworn with all their heart, and sought him with their whole desire; and he was found of them: and the Lord gave them rest round about.[99]

98. 2 Nephi 2:25.
99. 2 Chronicles 15:15.

CHAPTER 5

WHERE YOUR HEART IS, THERE WILL YOUR TREASURE BE ALSO

*S*hortly after my husband was released as bishop of our California ward, someone asked him what he had learned. He said there was a long list, but one thing he could share was this: there would be much less sin in the Church if no one considered themselves an exception.

Unfortunately, we do think of ourselves that way. We often hear it, and sometimes think it ourselves: "With my particular talent . . . with my particular yearnings . . . with my particular needs . . . well, the Lord understands. He won't keep me out of His presence for these things. He knows my heart."

He does indeed understand. As far as our heart is concerned—well, He is the only one who knows our hearts.[100] He knows them a whole lot better than we know our own.

Yes, He knows our hearts, but the determinative question is this: What kind of progress are we making toward knowing *His* heart? For the purpose of choosing whether we will seek to know Him and His heart, we have come to a fallen world to be enticed by good and/or evil. But just being here isn't enough. The only way we can know Him is to have good triumph over evil in our own heart. That's our choice.

We can define evil, as Mormon did,[101] as anything that takes us away from Christ. If we have preferences for anything that takes us away from our role in the Father's plan, we need a mighty change of heart.[102]

---

100. D&C 6:16.
101. Moroni 7:17–19.
102. Alma 34:31.

Our talents, yearnings, and needs must become less important to us than our love for our Father in Heaven. The things we want have so much good in them that it seems harsh to call them "evil." Perhaps I should find a better word, but I guess it is okay to use Mormon's word. After all, King Saul's posterity lost the throne of Israel because Saul wanted to use his own judgment as to what was good (and, in his view, a righteous sacrifice) instead of doing what the Lord had assigned him to do. What the prophet Samuel said to Saul is still true: "To obey is better than sacrifice."[103]

Somehow we have adopted a belief that God's love for us, and the good in what we have chosen outside of His will for us, will lead Him to broaden the path. He loves us so much that He will surely accommodate our exceptions. Surely, He will share our view of what we see as righteous preferences. We have come to believe that mercy means indulgence. "Surely," we tell ourselves, "He will broaden the path."

He says no, He can't. The path is governed by law[104] and must stay narrow.[105] However, eternal law has provided for accommodation of our good, but not celestial, preferences with lesser glories. It all depends upon what our hearts really prefer. Which path. Which glory.[106]

We all have the same purpose for coming to this earth. The purpose is to choose whether to know God the Eternal Father and His son Jesus Christ.[107] Still, there are a variety of missions. For that reason, we do not ignore the fact that there are truly exceptions from, for instance, the roles as stated in the family proclamation. Nevertheless, those exceptions are to be identified by the Lord. If it is our desire to prepare to live in the perfect love of our Father in Heaven, what is best for us cannot be simply the preference of our natural man.[108] We can believe that our happiness is in one direction, when our Father in Heaven knows it's in another. Sacrifice will always be an important principle toward our ultimate joy, because what we don't pay much for, we don't value as much. It is sacrifice that shows our heart to our Father in Heaven—and, incidentally, to ourselves. What we are willing to give up for our love is the great revealer

---

103. 1 Samuel 15.
104. D&C1 :31.
105. Matthew 7:14.
106. D&C 76.
107. 2 Nephi 2:25–26.
108. Proverbs 3:5–6.

of both our devotion and our choice. Our Father in Heaven knows what each of us must do and not do in order to be able to abide perfect and eternal love. He will tell us, and we must listen with our whole desire. It is important that we remember how to receive that direction. Ironically, it can come only when we are willing to not be an exception. *Sacrifice must be given as a matter of loving obedience, not as a substitute for it.*[109]

I do want to acknowledge that this validation of the spirit of which I speak is not for what has been called "every frivolous decision." I speak here of the life-changing decisions regarding our roles and missions. Both President Hinckley and President Oaks gave cautionary words about this in *Preach My Gospel*.[110]

The Spirit will give us "commandments not a few."[111] How grateful we can be for that information.

Unfortunately, it is not unusual for us to misidentify the Spirit when our own wants are intense. Perhaps the most common error in the identification of the Spirit is the belief that our desires themselves are the Spirit speaking to us. The question we must ask ourselves is "do we want His will more than anything, or are we too quick to be convinced that God is validating what we want?" The Spirit seldom speaks to an individual who doesn't deeply desire to know and do the will of the Lord.[112]

Many women are not given the opportunity for motherhood in this life. In order to prepare for eternal exalted motherhood, it is still incumbent upon them to choose to nurture in whatever else they do. That is how they show their hunger and thirst after righteousness.

In addition, many women with children must deal with circumstances that make it impossible to be stay-at-home mothers. Here again, it is important for us to identify the difference between being limited by circumstance and acting on our own preferences as a matter of seeking our own. Preference to have someone else raise our children is altogether different from circumstantial limitation. Children know when you are choosing to avoid being the one to influence their growing up. It simply is lesser love, lesser living of the list.

---

109. 1 Samuel 15:22.
110. *Preach My Gospel* (Salt Lake City: The Church of Jesus Christ of Latter-day Saints, 2018), 97.
111. D&C 59:4.
112. 3 Nephi 12:6.

If we can keep in mind that the most important thing our children can learn from us is how to love,[113] we will live a life that teaches it.[114] That learning is difficult for our children if it is not modeled for them. It requires our time and our trouble. It requires repeating ourselves a hundred times a day: "Say thank you to Mrs. Jones." "Don't throw the ball at Suzy." The decision is whether to stay with our children and do the tough stuff with love and devotion, or to choose a path with short-range pleasure. Whatever the will of the Lord for an individual, every God-given mission has this in common: we can't serve two masters. We can't have it all, no matter how true it is that in the beginning we think we can. The scriptures warn that it never ends up that way.[115]

A plea we often hear is this: "I'm not happy staying at home all day. I love my work and when I'm happy I'm a much better mother." I would agree that a happy woman makes a better mother. However, it has been my observation that when a woman's happiness depends upon being away from her children, she is teaching them precious little about how to love. Besides, her children know, even if she doesn't, that happiness is a choice. As Mary Ellen Edmunds used to tell our sister missionaries in the Missionary Training Center: " 'Be of good cheer.' This is not a suggestion."

We want our preferences to prevail whether or not the Spirit agrees. It becomes a matter of reasonability to us. If the sacrifice is not necessary, why do it? Trouble is, our assessment of what makes sense trusts in our arm of flesh.[116] We want our own reasonable plan of salvation. It amounts to believing that desire can rob sacrifice. It is much the same as believing that mercy can rob justice. As we have been told so often, mercy cannot rob justice.[117] And "reasonable" desire cannot rob sacrifice as a way to show our hearts to our Father in Heaven. Both are an attempt at indulgence instead of responsibility. Both want the path broadened because "God understands." Both lack faith and love.

The process of seeking to be perfectible always makes me think of John Henry Newman's lyrics in the hymn "Lead, Kindly Light."[118] He wrote, "I loved to choose and see my path; but now, lead thou me on!"

113. 1 Corinthians 13:1–2; Deuteronomy 6:5–7; 2 Nephi 25:23.
114. Matthew 22:39.
115. Matthew 6:24.
116. Jeremiah 17:5.
117. Alma to Corianton, Alma 42:8.
118. *Hymns*, no. 97.

Here on earth, we prepare for a kingdom of glory. Our priorities will determine the glory we are given. Wanting it so much that we prioritize it is what the Lord is looking for. That will be enough.[119] Overriding desire to be children of Christ will lead us to have a critical mass of love. Unfortunately, we are capable of kidding ourselves about that desire. Therefore, it is God's judgment of our desire that will be determinative.

The scriptures are replete with reminders that Christ came to do the will of His Father.[120] He would have liked to be relieved of the pain, but His priority was to do the assigned task: "If it be possible, let this cup pass from me: nevertheless, not as I will, but as thou wilt."[121] If we have come here to choose whether or not to know Christ, and if that knowing requires Christlike behavior, then we, too, will find our eternal joy in that "nevertheless."

If we want to get on that path of perfectibility, we must look past the worldly doctrine of "finding ourselves first," which is a popular, but dangerous, doctrine that makes us want to believe that we are exceptions. We must remember this principle of righteousness: Lose yourself for His sake to find yourself.[122]

When we were on our mission in Quebec, Elder F. Burton Howard was our Area President. Many times he told us and our missionaries that the most damaging words in our language are, "I've gotta be me!" I came to understand that he did not mean that it is not okay to be me. To think otherwise is ingratitude for the gifts of God. He simply meant that when we put ourselves, or our natural man, first (with all its talents, yearnings, and needs), we step off the perfectible path. We're still on a path to glory, but it is not a path to celestial glory. If we want a celestial eternity, change in "me" will be necessary.

God's love gives us unlimited opportunities to change and turn our hearts to Him as long as we are in this life. For some whose preferences will be seen by an all-wise judge to have been skewed by circumstance, they will have the opportunity to choose in the next world.[123]

If we have the opportunity to choose here, we must make ourselves into worthy servants. That means preparation for our mission is necessary.

---

119. D&C 88:21.
120. John 6:38.
121. Matthew 26:39.
122. Matthew 16:25–26.
123. See D&C 76:109–10.

In the process, however, wisdom dictates that we carefully should not become carried away into self-focus.

I spent some time recently with a young, returned missionary. She was enrolled at the university, and we were talking about her experience there. She said,

> It's so hard right after a mission. For eighteen months, I have lived completely out of myself. Every day was spent worrying about investigators or trying to find them. Now, all the sudden, it is all about me. I have to concentrate on myself—what I want to study, what I want to be. It just feels odd.

I asked her if I could help her with that. I told her that she was still on a mission. The preparation is part of the contribution she will make—as a wife and mother and as a member of her community. Nothing should ever be about self-focus. Whether we are in the preparation phase or in the serving stage, our focus must always be on the contribution if we are to fill our place in the plan of salvation.[124] That is the message the brethren intended to make us constantly aware of when they put up the sign at the entrance to Brigham Young University: "Enter to Learn, Go forth to Serve."

A short time after I spoke with that young woman, I read this verse in the Doctrine and Covenants, section 93, verse 53.

> And, verily I say unto you, that it is my will that you should hasten to translate my scriptures, and to obtain a knowledge of history, and of countries, and of kingdoms, of laws of God and man. And all this for the salvation of Zion. Amen.

It is the Lord's directive to the prophet Joseph, but for those of us who want to fill our part in the plan of salvation, we can take it for ourselves as well. We will likely not be called on to translate, but if we change that word to "study," we are pretty close to an admonishment to all of us. We must prepare for whatever the mission is that has been revealed to us. Then we must carry it out. The important thing to remember is that all of it is for the salvation of Zion.

---

124. See D&C 38:30.

The same is true about having the energy to do the Lord's work. Energy production will be necessary. The time we spend with rest and recreation can be delightful. It is easy to think of these things as an end in themselves. If we are to keep our eye single to eternal life, even our R & R can be done with the motivation to be better servants. Paradoxically, everything that helps us maintain that focus will bring us more joyful energy. That's because of the love that will accompany our dedication. When real love is involved, we aren't worried about giving too much. Limiting and measuring uses up the most energy.

The only way to get ultimate glory is to, as King Benjamin taught us, be submissive, meek, humble, full of love, and all those other attributes of godliness that appear on the list.[125] Going after glory directly will limit our glory to a lesser kingdom than the one where God the Father dwells. That is the law that determines our eternity. It's a paradox to be sure.

> And they who are not sanctified through the law which I have given unto you, even the Law of Christ, must inherit another kingdom, even that of a terrestrial kingdom, or that of a telestial kingdom.[126]

It is one big paradox, isn't it? The perfect place for us to make the perfectible choices is in a fallen, imperfect world. We look around without God's perspective and see everything as imperfect. He looks and sees a perfection of opposition and enticings in which we can know what it is we really want to choose. Both our agency and opposition are at work.[127]

Everything in scripture and from our prophets tells us what to strive for if we want, on resurrection morning, to rise to a celestial glory. It can only happen if we have learned to abide a portion of the celestial law, and that law requires living the list, embracing our roles and missions. Our patriarchal blessings and other visitations of the Spirit will make our individual missions clear. But because there are competing timetables, we must be sure to understand which missions come first. We women, if we are given the influential and ideal role in the plan, can recognize it as an indispensable and therefore priority role to play. Because, you see,

---

125. Mosiah 3:19.
126. D&C 88:21–22.
127. 2 Nephi 2.

its priority is our Father in Heaven. It is our part in the plan of salvation. Or, in other words, parenthood is a missionary effort.

> Therefore, O ye that embark in the service of God, see that ye serve him with all your heart, might, mind and strength, that ye may stand blameless before God at the last day. . . . And faith, hope, charity and love, with an eye single to the glory of God, qualify [us] for the work. Remember faith, virtue, knowledge, temperance, patience, brotherly kindness, godliness, charity, humility, diligence.[128]

---

128. D&C 4:2, 5–6.

PART 2

BARRIERS TO THE BEST CHOICES

For it must needs be, that there
is an opposition in all things.

—2 Nephi 2:11

CHAPTER 6

VISIBILITY—A TOUGH SACRIFICE

While summer traveling with our children and grandchildren many years ago, we took the little ones to a wonderfully creative park to play. They loved it. They ran randomly from slide to rope bridge and from locomotive to ladders. Everything they tried was accompanied by squeals of "Mama, Daddy, Grandy, Papa, watch me! Watch me!" And we did. We loved it too.

Eventually the younger family went to try the paddle boats, and my husband and I sat on a bench, still in the playground. After a bit, a long, well-ordered line of children entered the park. Supervising teenagers walked next to them at intervals of about every ten feet. After they entered the park, the teenagers divided the children into groups and assigned them to "turns" on the different play equipment. When a whistle was blown, they changed devices. The children yelled at one another—some in pleasure, some in pain—so there was noise. We watched and listened to them. My husband said to me, "Can you hear it?" I didn't know what he meant, so he explained, "There is no 'watch me watch me.'"

My heart suddenly ached for those regimented little sweethearts. Children should be able to feel like the center of somebody's universe. It is the way their little souls can begin to understand how God feels about them. Their lives should be full of "Watch me! Watch me!"

It's easier to understand that we are our Savior's "whole work and glory" when we have occupied that role with earthly list-living parents. When our mama has been available at every little hurt to "kiss it better," it is much easier to understand that "by His stripes we are healed."[129] When we have been able to cry out to be watched in our little triumphs, we may be able to feel more comfortable asking our Father in Heaven to watch out for us in our big efforts.

It is indeed the role of the parent to prepare the child to know the Lord.

Engraved in my memory is an incident that happened in our home when my oldest boy was two or three. I had carelessly put some excess rug shampoo in a drinking glass, and its bright color was irresistible to my child. It was in a drinking glass. He thought it was a drink. He drank it. When I discovered it, I was panicked! I'm not one who deals with crisis well. I thought he was going to die! And because I thought it, so did he. He was a little upset, but nowhere nearly as upset as I was.

"Mama," he said. "Will Heavenly Father give me a hug right away as soon as I get there?"

I was deeply touched. I took my little boy into my arms. "Oh yes!" I said. "If you have to go, He will be there." I have been led by my child's reassurance[130] ever since.

I think perhaps the peace that can come to a "watch me, watch me" child can help when that child must transition to adulthood. There will come a time when he will need to be able to take his "turn" at making others the center of his universe. Loving and understanding are intended to be perpetually given. We mature, take the name of the Lord upon us, and commit to extend and expand His work and glory among our fellows.[131] When we become adults, the center of our universe needs to be the children of God—whether they are our own children or someone else's. If we have our own children, they constitute a particular commandment to be kept,[132] but if we don't, the mission of adulthood will still come. That mission is to develop the "attributes of godliness."

But here's the problem: we all grow into adults physically, but we don't all "grow up" spiritually. Whether we had perfect or imperfect childhoods, the maturity is still a matter of choosing to grow into the Lord's definition of love. Having an early loving start makes it easier, but it can be done the hard way—which is usually the case. The adult "how

---

129. Isaiah 53:5.
130. Isaiah 11:6.
131. Dallin H. Oaks, *His Holy Name* (Salt Lake City: Deseret Book, 2009), 19.
132. Deuteronomy 6:7.

to" is available to us but is very different from how we may have gained a foundation of understanding as children. It's almost polar opposite. What we *received* as children (if we were lucky) must now be *given*.

The learning method of children is simply not available to grown-ups. The mature choice to know Christ requires giving up "watch me, watch me." Oh, God is still watching us, all right, but an adult does not have the natural humility that a child has. There is a kind of acknowledged affection in a child's giving us the gift of seeing him perform. As adults, our cry to "watch me, watch me" does not, and cannot, have the innocence of a child. It is no longer, "I know you love me and I want to make you proud." In adults, it is more like, "I want you to admire me so that *I* can be proud." It's a significant difference. With those "watch me, watch me" words, a child is acknowledging love. In an adult, that attitude is saying, "You don't admire me enough." It's hard for us to accept that our striving for validation of our pride may be wrong. We would like to know Christ from that lovely childlike way. We would like to get attention with just that kind of innocence. We even tell ourselves that it will still work the way it does for children. We tell ourselves that what we see as a need is justified because we must "find ourselves." I'm afraid that finding self—if not done as a child—must be achieved by "losing self" as adults. That is the only way an adult can make the "finding" happen. That is because, paradoxically, developing the humility to "become as little children"[133] is a matter of becoming *Christ's* little children, not at all the same as being the little children we became when we were born into the world. We cannot even begin to understand what it means to be Christ's little children without first living "the list," and that is a very adult endeavor.

We may be trying to hold on to a child's learning method—that of feeling loved and nurtured, which we joyfully experienced. We may be trying to capture the security we never knew. It amounts to the same disability. That disability is pride, and pride makes it impossible to progress toward knowing the Lord. It's a paradox that the desires of a humble child translate into the pride of an adult, but like many paradoxes, it's reality. To become Christ's little children, we must "put away childish things."[134]

---

133. Matthew 18:3.
134. 1 Corinthians 13:11.

My ache for those little regimented sweethearts in the park was that they were not learning the way only a child can. They were not learning what it is like to have the dawn of security. That dawn is an early association with focused love. Those squealing childhood moments do help us see what God's caring for us must be like. As adults, we must get that understanding from taking upon us His name and His mission. We must *give* the pure love of Christ in order to experience it. And oh, it is so worth it!

Seeing the need and not understanding, our society has tried to make self-esteem a substitute for experiencing that security. It won't work. That security comes from knowing the depth of God's love. One cannot give it to one's self.[135] Even if one has devoted love from an earthly source, ultimately one must still get it from God. And one must do that by choosing to receive it. The choice is made by putting one's full effort into living the "principles of righteousness."

Somewhere along the line, no matter our disadvantages, each of us can make the decision to work toward those principles. In so doing, we will know God and feel of His love directly from His heart to ours. We will know then the meaning of Lehi's dream and why Nephi called the fruit of the tree of life the "most desirable above all things."[136] The chain reaction of perfectibility will have begun.

Our roles are given us in order to make that process possible. It is rarely the visible roles that yield us pure knowledge. The iron rod is not inside the spacious building. Lehi and Nephi knew the taste of the pure fruit, and they wanted their family to partake.[137] In our inadequate human condition, few can define love let alone taste of it. But that iron rod (the word of God) can help with both, because that's where we find "the list." Whether it be in the scriptures, conference addresses, or in the revelations of the Spirit, it is "the word of God—the iron rod."[138] The word of God will always tell us to live "the list," and when we do, we will always want our family to partake of the delicious fruit thereof. As a result, we will do whatever is necessary to help them taste of it.

The Lord has used so many different metaphors to help us understand these basics of the gospel. The pure, self-sacrificing love of God and

---

135. Matthew 15:25.
136. 1 Nephi 11:22.
137. 1 Nephi 8:12.
138. See D&C 1:38.

our fellows is the oil in our lamps.[139] It is the table prepared beside the still waters.[140] It is, as we will point to throughout this book, the pearl of great price.[141] And so many more. How thrilling that He has told us how to work toward feeling that love.

Trying to get the security of knowing Christ in immature ways is futile. It's like God is telling us in accents sweet: Dear ones, it won't work. Not anymore.

As Paul concluded his rendering of the list, he acknowledged that it is different from what a child is and does. Some things are appropriate when one is a child, but Paul reminded us that "When I became a man I put away childish things."[142] That statement puts the whole list in focus. The list is of what an adult must do (almost always in private and without visibility) to experience pure love. If the virgin is ready for the bridegroom, she will have the oil of the Spirit in her lamp. That comes from the maturity of *giving* godlike love.

The virgin with the empty lamp[143] has not yet (if I might mix the scriptural metaphors) tasted of the fruit. She is still trying to be a child and is definitely not ready for the wedding. The list as it is given, is a description of a *security-giving* member of God's task force. The difference in the method of coming closer to God is to enter into the paradox that the greatest among us must become servants.[144] Clearly, it is taking His yoke of love upon us, which helps us learn of Him,[145] whether we had that opportunity to connect with His love as a child or not. It is hard, but we can do hard.

For myself I find I cannot truthfully make the claim that Paul makes. I cannot put away childish things. At least not enough to stop me from seeing through a glass darkly most of the time.[146] Nevertheless, knowing that the goal is to turn away from self-serving can help all of us to have glimpses of understanding of our God. Line upon line those glimpses can move us along the path. Being on that path is what can

---

139. Matthew 25.
140. Psalm 23.
141. Matthew 13:45–46.
142. 1 Corinthians 13:11.
143. Matthew 25; 1 Nephi 8.
144. Matthew 23:11–15.
145. Matthew 11:29.
146. 1 Corinthians 13:12.

make us eligible to be perfected in Christ.[147] As the Psalmist said, "Thou wilt shew me the path of life: in thy presence is fulness of joy" (Psalms 16:11).

The method of learning taught by the scriptures as being the only way is, in reality, the easy yoke and the light burden. Nevertheless, most of us have enough of our unconquered natural man in us that "visibility" becomes a difficult sacrifice indeed. That's why it is rarely achieved. We keep beating the horse of trying to get it in the childlike way. We may not be so noisy as a child at the park squealing, "Watch me! Watch me!" but we do seek recognition and credit. Being "seen of men" is important to us. We seek our own, and we vaunt ourselves.[148]

Sacrificing our visibility is tough, and yet that sacrifice is probably a defining surrender.

If we were to travel the easy road of the natural man, it would not lead us, as adults, to know the value of eternal life. The very fact of its difficulty is part of the exercise we have come to a fallen world to experience. Believe it or not, the fact of its being hard is what makes it possible. As Lehi said it: "Adam fell that men might be; and men are, that they might have joy."[149] As President Nelson has said: It is the joy of Jesus Christ that we were created to feel.[150]

Joseph Smith said that we must learn the character of God.[151] Moroni said that we must deny ourselves of ungodliness.[152] The scriptures make it clear to us what God's character is, and therefore its opposite: ungodliness. That opposite is what we must deny ourselves. They also make it clear that the rewards God has to offer combine together to bring eternal joy. That eternal joy will be perfect love.

That eternal perfect love will be the result of our gradually rising to a perfectible critical mass of it through our agency. We can start that chain reaction of love and so receive a celestial perfection of it when Christ completes us. It is only through the perfecting power of His Atonement that we, who came so slowly to our critical mass, will be able to abide

---

147. See Moroni 10:31.
148. 1 Corinthians 13.
149. 2 Nephi 2:25.
150. Russell M. Nelson, "Drawing the Power of Jesus Christ into Our Lives," *Ensign*, May 2017.
151. Smith, *Lectures on Faith*, 3.
152. Moroni 10:32.

perfect love forever. I am frequently reminded again of Paul when he told us, "If in this life only we have hope in Christ, ye are of all men most miserable."[153]

That is because in this life, our love is incomplete. Visibility actually becomes a temporary substitute for it. I believe that is what the Savior was addressing in the Sermon on the Mount:

> But when thou doest alms, let not thy left hand know what thy right hand doeth:
>
> That thine alms may be in secret: and thy Father which seeth in secret himself shall reward thee openly.
>
> And when thou prayest, thou shalt not be as the hypocrites are: for they love to pray standing in the synagogues and in the corners of the streets, that they may be seen of men. Verily I say unto you, They have their reward.[154]

I believe that when the Lord said, "they have their reward," He was acknowledging (as was Lehi with his "enticement" terminology[155]) that the visibility among our fellow humans is indeed rewarding in the moment. He is also telling us that in order to achieve the eternal and open reward, the "seen of men" reward must be sacrificed. It is left to us to decide which reward we want—the transitory attention that we get from visibility, or the great and eternal love that can be ours forever. The small nuggets of reward invisibility cannot give us the critical mass of love that can make us perfectible. Only that which I call "the list" can do that.[156]

It turns out that something happens within us when we are willing to take the Lord's mission of self-sacrifice as our own. That happening is profound. It is the same "worth it" change that we talk of in other chapters of this book. It's called a "mighty change of heart."[157] It's called a "broken heart and a contrite spirit."[158] It is the transformation that can come to grown-ups when they learn and return the love of the Lord by

---

153. 1 Corinthians 15:19.
154. Matthew 6:3–5.
155. 2 Nephi 2:16.
156. 1 John 4:7–8.
157. Mosiah 5:2.
158. 2 Nephi 2:7.

following directions. It's a choice. Our choices are the foundation of our eternity.

"Putting away childish things," especially regarding how we seek God's love, is as hard as anything our natural man will ever do. But we must keep trying if we want to bask eternally in that love. It takes singleness of purpose to reach a critical mass of love. Remember, that for which we have not paid much will not mean much. The critical mass of love requires the kind of focus for which a great price is happily paid.

Matthew chapter 13 tells the tale of that pearl of great price. It is the parable of the merchant who had many pearls to sell, but when he had the opportunity to buy one beautiful pearl of great price, he sold all the other pearls to buy it. The giving of the pure love of Christ stands alone as the pearl of greatest price. We have to believe that it is worth surrendering those little pearls. Our reach toward that purchase *is* the critical mass of love.

> And thou shalt love the Lord thy God with all thine heart, and with all thy soul, and with all thy might.
>
> And these words, which I command thee this day, shall be in thine heart:
>
> And thou shalt teach them diligently unto thy children, and shalt talk of them when thou sittest in thine house, and when thou walkest by the way, and when thou liest down, and when thou risest up.[159]

---

159. Deuteronomy 6:5–7.

CHAPTER 7

EYE SINGLE VS. HAVING IT ALL

*M*y husband graduated from medical school sixty years ago. During his internship year, it was time to decide if he would "specialize."

He chose radiology. At that time, to be boarded in radiology meant that you were "certified" to practice in diagnostic radiology, all of what they called "radiation therapy," and the fledgling specialty of "nuclear medicine." It wasn't long before it was determined that nuclear medicine required more exclusive focus, and nuclear medicine was split off from the broader specialty. Eventually, radiation therapy began to be called radiation oncology, and it, too, was separated off so that the excellence that comes from focus could be achieved. Near the time of my husband's retirement, diagnostic radiology was also divided up. Interventional radiology was separated from the mother ship.

In these past decades, my husband's field is not the only one to acknowledge that expertise is stronger in specialization. Allowing a more directed focus allows for more knowledge, experience, and a greater contribution.

During these same decades, however, married feminists have been preaching an opposite doctrine. During these same decades, when many of them have participated in this fever of specialization in the workplace, they have both preached and practiced a belief that as far as the home is concerned, there can be a thinning of the focus instead of a concentration of it. I've heard it called "balance." No need for specialization of homemaking. No need to "spin-off" from other activities. Either it is believed that focus on family is unnecessary, or that it is easily delegated. It amounts to believing that choice is unnecessary. In their belief that there is no need for choice in this fundamental role of the plan of salvation, they are experiencing a misunderstanding about the purpose of this life. Still, they find ways to believe they have it right. Some may even tell themselves that they are sending their children off to "specialists" when they send them off to day care. However, inasmuch as the most important thing we are to teach our children is how to love, those "specialists" in teaching skills and manners still leave a deficit that only a devoted mother can fill.

In the 1990s, I wrote a book for the organization "American Mothers." I did seminars on mothering for them for a while. On one such occasion, a young woman approached me after the class and said,

> My mother always worked outside the home. I work outside the home as well. Until tonight, I always wondered why the leaders of my Church recommended that a mother stay at home. Until tonight, I thought staying home meant wasting time babysitting. Do you really believe what you said tonight about a child needing the power of our influence?

I answered that I believe it with all my heart. Then, since we shared our faith, I continued, "They need to be central to our mortal mission, as we are central to the Savior's. They need us to love them as we have been loved. They cannot feel that introduction to the love of the Lord if they are squeezed in on holidays."

I hastened to add that should a mother need to work outside the home to support her family (and this is far too often true), her working does not divide her focus. It is evidence of it. Such evidence is not lost on her children. They feel that central position in her focus. But when a woman works outside the home because for whatever reason she prefers it—well, the children feel that too. They are not then the center of their mother's consecration to her Father in Heaven, and they know it.

If they have a loving and long-term nanny, they will be somewhat less damaged, but the nanny's influence is raising the children, not the mother's. The most important service being done in that home is by that influential figure, not by the woman who chose the rewards of leaving the home instead of the rewards of focusing on the home. It will not be only that the nanny's influence will be what blesses the children, but she is also the one who will have eternal blessings because of it. That's the way it works. When a child has had an environment of love, it opens that child's mind and heart to the influence of that caregiver. Not only that, but love (or the lack of it) also tends to be reciprocal. Since both influence and love have an eternal place in us, that nanny will have an eternal relationship that will bring great blessings. But in truth, I'm probably wishful thinking anyway. The value of a long-term, loving nanny is probably a moot point. I suspect that it's rare when a career mother has a long-term, loving nanny. The mother may call them nannies, but in truth, a revolving door of babysitters and day care centers is more likely.

Still, even a long termer is a sad option. I remember years ago reading an article in a magazine written by an anonymous male. He omitted his name, because, should his wife have discovered the article, he would have had to deal with some serious marital discord.

The couple had two children. Both he and his wife were employed outside the home. He said that his income was more than adequate but that his wife felt "better about herself" when she worked, as she did, in middle management of a mid-sized company. He said that he and his wife were Southern European Jews but that an Irish Catholic nanny was raising their children. He mourned that his children were being raised with altogether different values than those of him and his wife. He reported that his wife was quick to reassure him that the weekends were for quality time with the children. In his view, though, she was not being honest with herself, "Because," he said, "that is the time we play tennis with friends and have a social life for the two of us." He was concerned since it amounted to very few quality hours for the children. He loved his wife and thought she could have been a wonderful influence on the children.

The first time I read that article, I cried—for the children, yes, but more for the mother. She chose to sacrifice the greatest potential she possessed. The focus on her career, I'm sure, was delightfully rewarding, but when it was over, so was the reward.

I'm sure she sang the song that we hear from so many women: "I know some women like to be at home, but it just isn't enough for me." I always smile at that comment, because the reason cannot be that it isn't enough. It is the hardest and most challenging job there is. Had she said, "It's just too much for me" it would have been more honest. Most honest of all would be to admit that it requires more self-sacrifice than many are willing to give.

I'm going to insert here the remarks of a young mother whose brutal honesty supports my observations. Note, however, that her love and goals make her sacrifice worth it. Note, too, that through her sacrifice she comes to know Christ, which is what the scriptures tell us makes anything and everything worth it.[160] Without that knowledge, we arrive at the bridegroom's coming with no oil in our lamps.[161]

Had the young mother whose words are below chosen to escape the tough stuff, I suppose it doesn't matter whether this young mother had convinced herself that it was "not enough" or that it was "too much." In any case, the real goal for coming to this fallen world would have been lost to her. She would simply have chosen a lesser reward.

> I'm lying on the floor in my bedroom. Tears are streaming over my temples and into my strewn-out hair. My kids are running around doing something that sounds a lot like dumping ice from the dispenser onto the kitchen floor. I don't know why I'm crying really. Maybe it's just a combination of it all.
>
> When I was little, I used to get frightened when I would see my mom cry. I remember only once or twice when she just lost it. She started sobbing and left the house, saying she'd be back in a few hours when she could stand to be home again. I never understood what she was so upset about. Undoubtedly she would return home with a much calmer demeanor, usually with nothing in hand after she had "gone shopping."
>
> I get it now. I just want to get away. I want all my possessions and surroundings to melt into the floor and I want to be alone. Well, maybe not alone. I just want to be with Christ. He is the only one who really gets me. I'm so tired of hearing little noises, little feet. I'm tired of wiping snotty noses and cleaning poop out of underwear and off the bathroom rug. I'm tired of trying to be kind while being yelled at by my tyrannical three-year-old. I just want one "thank you!" I keep asking myself, "Does anyone appreciate me?" And before I can even finish the question, I feel my soul being whipped back around, and my chest starts pounding. "I do," Christ says. "I hear you. I know,"

---

160. John 17:3.
161. Matthew 25:2–13.

He always replies. He is the constant in my ever-changing world of emotions.

My kids come in the room asking me for a snack. They notice my face is red and my makeup looks like it's three days old. They stop suddenly in the doorway, not sure what to say or ask. They hesitantly ask for a snack. I yell back. "I don't care! Just leave me alone for a few minutes!"

Gosh. Why did I yell at them? They didn't do anything. I'm a terrible mom. I hope no one comes to the door right now. I look like a mess. It would be embarrassing to not look put-together if someone from the ward popped by. They would ask me what's wrong, and then I'd have to lie through my teeth, saying I was fine when I'm really not, but I have too many words to say to explain it, and yet there's nothing to explain. Then I'd just have to smile and keep acting like everything is perfect like everyone does at Church.

Why do I feel this way? It's like I'm having to find things in my life that are "not ideal" so I can sit and nitpick them into an actual problem. That way when my husband gets home and asks me why I'm so quiet, I have something to say. Maybe it's the day to day. Maybe it's that we just moved here and I have no real friends yet and I feel alone. Maybe it's the fact that I keep posting things on Instagram to get some satisfaction, and I'm just now realizing that all those comments make me feel worse. Even the kind comments are just shallow niceties that leave me feeling hallow and wanting more validation. Maybe it's that my one-year-old hasn't slept through the night since she was born. Or maybe it's that I feel a small tickle in my throat and I'm catching that cold that's going around. Maybe I'm feeling down because my kids do not like their new school and my seven-year-old comes home crying because his teacher yelled at him for forgetting his homework, the homework I forgot to sign and put in his backpack. I don't know. Maybe it's all of those things combined. Or maybe none of them at all, really.

My three-year-old walks up the stairs bawling his eyes out like his arm got cut off because he is sad that his brother opened the door that he wanted to open. Heaven forbid. God give me patience.

I want to close my eyes, shut it all out, and escape for a while. Not a long time. Just long enough to realize how good my life is, to step back and really miss my babies. I want to leave my messy house and come back grateful that I have a house to clean, to realize that I don't want or need validation from other people. The only person I need validation from is Him, the Peacegiver.

But first I must ask for forgiveness. I am selfish, Lord. I'm a spoiled imp who doesn't deserve this fine life I've been given. Give me strength to get off this floor, to wipe the tears off my temples, and brush my hair. Help me rise above my own demons. Help me be strong and kind. Help me to go to my two-year-old's room with quiet patience and love.

Oh my gosh. I understand now. I am my two-year-old, crying over stupid, inconsequential things to a parent who was just trying to help me. He was trying to teach me, and all I did was cry and whine over all these "hard things." And to think, I never thanked Him.

Isn't it interesting that the world was so slow to figure out what the Lord has always taught us about focus. The "eye single to God and His glory" is the best motivation and the only real solace.[162]

And faith, hope, charity and love, with an eye single to the glory of God, qualify him for the work.

Remember faith, virtue, knowledge, temperance, patience, brotherly kindness, godliness, charity, humility, diligence.[163]

And thou shalt love the Lord thy God with all thine heart, and with all thy soul, and with all thy might.

And these words, which I command thee this day, shall be in thine heart:

And thou shalt teach them diligently unto thy children, and shalt talk of them when thou sittest in thine house, and when thou walkest by the way, and when thou liest down, and when thou risest up.[164]

---

162. Matthew 6:22; D&C 4:5.
163. D&C 4:5–6.
164. Deuteronomy 6:5–7.

CHAPTER 8

MEN ARE FROM EARTH
(AND SO ARE WOMEN)

*H*ow in the world did all these concerns that the world calls "women's issues" begin? Well, no, let's not go back that far! I'm content to just look to the sixties when I first started thinking about it.

A lot was going on at the United Nations. A Swedish woman named Alva Myrdahl was pushing what she called "equal rights" there. Few Americans were aware of it. In the United States, Betty Friedan caused significant upheaval about the problem and was the one who suggested "liberation" as a solution. Then there were those women who read her work and were driven by it. Of course, "there is no new thing under the sun."[165] They weren't the first to find frustration in their role. Without understanding of the importance of the plan of salvation, the frustration is inevitable. It is, after all, a fallen world. All those folks did was to come up with a revolutionary and counter-list, counter-loving solution.

No, the problem is not new. Even the "liberation" solution had been tried before—but mostly on the individual level. In the sixties, it became a collective and loud shout. It was not just frustration; it was resentment. I think we must acknowledge that there were reasons it snowballed.

Generally, women in the hands-on role of stay-at-home mothers were undervalued (both the women and their missions) by their husbands, friends, and subsequently in their own eyes. It caused a depth of self-focus that can only result in self-pity. And so, forgetting "the first law of holes" (when you are in one, stop digging), women were in a hole and kept digging. Instead of finding ways to testify for and plead the

---

165. Ecclesiastes 1:9.

valuation of our role, we bought into its undervaluing and wanted to abandon it. We wanted to be more like the women who were valued by our husbands and by our society. Women wanted to leave the home and have what their husbands seemed to want more than a mother's influence on their children. What Betty Friedan and other authors did was to make it sound like that was okay and that it was the right thing to do. Even the government got on board and made laws that favored women who worked outside the home.

Because some men undervalued the full-time nurturing role and overvalued material things, they encouraged their wives to bring in extra income. Because some men's eyes tended to linger on the well-put-together women at work, women wanted to be those girls who didn't have babies pulling at their hair, rubbing up against their makeup, and spitting up all over their clothes.

I remember a cartoon strip back in the early sixties that expressed it well. In the first frame, the husband says to his frazzled wife: "Why can't you look like Jackie Kennedy? She's so chic." The next frame showed smoke coming out of his wife's ears and forehead. "Darling," she said, "You hire me a cook and a housekeeper. Then hire a live-in hairdresser. Then hire me a designer that specializes in designing clothes just for me. Then, Darling, I'll smother you in chic!"

If it wasn't the income or the physical appearance, it was an intellectual complaint or any number of other put-downs. Like sheep, many women followed the unloving leaders to find a way to be valued. It was, in terms of eternity, a self-defeating error.

While ultimately we must get love and confidence from our Father in Heaven, it is no accident that He put us here as social creatures. God intended us to love one another.[166] He wanted us to give each other a knowledge of our value. He wanted us to introduce one another to the pure love of Christ (particularly in our marriages and family life). Although a full adult knowledge and understanding of that love can only be achieved by giving it, we can still make it easier for one another to give by helping others see the joyful example of it.

While our godly development depends on our being the giver, it is important to understand that blessings come in sets of two or more. Shakespeare still had it right when he agreed with Solomon: It blesses

---

166. Matthew 22:39.

those who give and those who take.[167] Men and women need to love one another and value one another's role. Both need to be grateful that they, too, can live a role that has a major influence for good in the plan of salvation.

When the Lord gave what some have called the curse to Adam and Eve at the Fall, He told women, "Your desire shall be to your husband."[168] I find that one of the most profound of the fallen world conditions.

In the first place, it has been true. For women, their desire is most often to their husbands, whether they have one or not. So, for single women this is a tough one. Although brides don't anticipate it, it turns out to be tough for married women as well. They want to live up to expectations, and they want their husbands' approbation for it. So what happens if their husbands' desire is contrary to other expectations? It happens a lot. So what then? Rarely good things. For instance, even though women are given the responsibility to receive their own witness of righteousness from the Holy Ghost,[169] they mistakenly believe that the God-given role is to blindly follow. Some try to live that way, but it doesn't work. It doesn't get them any more of their husband's love or their own well-being. So what happens next? They resent their desire being to their husbands, and they either deny it, fight it, or do both. Wanting to find one's activity outside the house is often a first thought. Some have even called the home a prison.

The irony is that women have tried to become the women their husbands look up to. They are following their husband's desires, and yet they are telling themselves that they have been liberated from them. They end up liberated only from the role that can produce the power of influence and eternal glory.[170] How much more free they would feel if they bore their testimony of the Lord's assigned roles and persuaded their husbands to want both of their roles filled. Women do have influence with their husbands.

The human condition is to need to be loved and valued, which includes both men and women. Many of us have lost sight of how that

---

167. William Shakespeare, *The Merchant of Venice*, act IV, scene 1; Proverbs 11:25–31.
168. Genesis 3:16.
169. Alma 56:48.
170. Moses 5:11.

joyful state can be found. We often find ourselves on paths that are counter to it.

The central event in the Garden of Eden involved Eve's acceptance of and valuing of her role. Next had to come the persuading of Adam that it was important enough for both of them to leave the Garden. It would not have served either of the necessary purposes of the creation[171] if Eve had left the garden without Adam. The plan required that man and woman become one and that they multiply and replenish the earth.[172] Both purposes require both taking responsibility. So Adam had to follow. The persuasion of a man by a woman can still be necessary. If it is, then we women must persuade. If men undervalue women's heaven-sent role, a woman can remember that in the garden the decision was made by Eve before Adam made it. I am always a little amused when our society talks of women's choice. It was and is women's choice—but the choice was made by Eve before conception, as it must be by us as well. Once her righteous choice to bear a family is made, that is the time for a woman's testimony to be borne and her commitment to be expressed. It is hoped that then man will see that it must be so. That conversation I'm sure has been played out in many a marriage. Sometimes, of course, the man first sees the value, but the woman still must decide, and they both must take responsibility. The mutual respect that this requires is often absent, and not just in the formation of families.

It's helpful here for me to retell something that happened to me a few decades ago. It illustrates this undervaluing of women that has led to women following those who suggest a counter-productive path. It brings a view of the world women lived in. It's actually two stories: two different men, two different views of women. The first view was the more prevalent in that society.

My husband and I attended a banquet with mostly other doctors and their wives. The man I sat next to was a vascular surgeon. I forget the initial conversation, but his response to it was this: "I'm glad I married a nurse. Only a nurse could realize that she is second place to my profession. She has to be, and she understands that."

I was horrified! I said, "John (not his name), shame on you! Poor Mary!"

---

171. 1 Corinthians 11:11; 2 Nephi 2:25.
172. Ibid.

"Well," said John, "let me tell you a story that illustrates this, and you will not be able to deny that she has to be second place. We were having a dinner party with twelve acquaintances at the house, many of whom Mary did not know well. I received a phone call about an emergency that only my expertise could handle. I was not on call, but I was needed. So, I left her with the party and went to the hospital. She had to be second place to my work. That's all there was to it."

"Oh, John," I answered, "I don't see it that way at all. You and Mary are one unit that had two jobs to do that night. You went to the hospital and did one of them, and she stayed home and did the other. When the day was done, you could report to one another that the two of you were successful in doing what your family unit was called upon to do. You made it all happen together. John, I've been a doctor's wife for a while now, and those incidents are not rare. You have to realize that it's a matter of working together to make good come about."

"Well, she's second place to me and my work. That's all there is to it!"

He was immovable, so I fell silent. In my quiet, I thought about an incident that had happened some years before. My husband had a patient who was critical and in danger. She was a middle-aged woman who had no family. He stayed at the hospital and sat at her bedside all night. She made it through the tough night, and in the morning, when she could speak, she was aware that my husband had been there. She thanked him and said, "You must be single too."

"No," he said, "I have a wife and two little boys."

"Oh my goodness! She'll hate you for this! I'm so sorry!"

"I don't think so," my husband answered. "She'll love that I was able to give you some comfort. She was part of the giving by my being here. That will make her happy."

It's tempting to say that these incidents show a difference in the women (especially because I am one of the women), but that would not be accurate. The difference is in the men and how they felt about the importance of their wives. My husband made me feel a part of his contributions, and he knew he was part of mine. Neither of us could have made a difference in our world without one another. The surgeon at the banquet needed a mighty change of heart. An attitudinal change in how he saw his wife's role and partnership. An understanding of the plan of salvation might have helped.

The unity of a married couple can happily be fashioned after the oneness of Christ and His Father. It is akin to the oneness that Christ prayed to His Father that we could achieve as a people.[173] Our sealing ordinances actually require eternal unity. It's hard to imagine God the Father considering His Son, Jesus Christ, as "second class" or second place. Likewise, it is impossible to think that Christ would consider doing the will of the Father to be demeaning. On the contrary. It is also hard to picture God the Father turning away from the petitions of His beloved Son. They are truly one.

The whole business of women being considered second place, second rate, second class—well, it created a climate where women just plain had to do something. Unfortunately, they chose badly. And now the change it has made in both men and women is not for the better. As society has tried to solve the problem by eliminating the roles, the anxiety has increased—not decreased. Faced with women who wanted sameness, many men have seen it as an escape from their own roles. Some have become less responsible in providing. Many live with women to whom they make no marriage commitment. Many children are born out of wedlock, and therefore outside of a sealed family chain. There is even a fear of dating, let alone accepting the responsibility of being a father. Men, too, landed in a hole. They, too, kept digging. Women in their resentment, in rejecting their desire being to their husbands, have managed to confuse some men and anger others. The result is a payback to men that has lessened women as well as men. Women have forfeited their influence, and men have forfeited their leadership.

To boys, men, husbands, and sons, may I please presume to give you advice: It's never too late. If you are blessed enough to have in your home a woman who has chosen to live the role of influence and nurturing, *hallow her choice*. Be enormously grateful that in this society that condescends to her, she has seen what she can do at home for you and your children and has called it more important than anything else. In return, I can almost promise you that she will find joy in her desire being to you.

Husbands, you are given a great example in father Adam. When given the opportunity to name this beautiful helpmeet that God had given him, he called her Eve. He said it was because she was the mother of all living.[174] The giving and taking on of names is essentially important in

---

173. See John 17:21 and Mark 10:8.
174. Genesis 3:20.

the ordinances of God's plan. When Adam gave that name to his wife, it was like a setting apart to be of prime importance in the world that was to come. Keep in mind that Eve's influence and persuasion caused the choice that men might be. They recognized that their roles—both of them—were key to the plan.

Women, I have advice for you too. Be willing to be the self-sacrificing nurturers that God intended, whether you are single or married, fertile or barren. That is what Eve agreed to, and we must follow. Again, it is paradoxical. We sacrifice ourselves and we find ourselves. To have a critical mass of love, there is no other way. We have made covenants to be worthy daughters of Eve.

Men, it is imperative that you have ordinancial respect for a woman's role and multiply that respect for her willingness to fill it.

> Most of all, men and women, let us love one another enough to become one.
>
> And Eve, also, his wife did labor with him. . . .
>
> And Adam and Eve, his wife, called upon the name of the Lord, and *they* heard the voice of the Lord.[175]

As you read this verse, please think of a woman's breast as a symbol for a mother's nurture.

> Let thy fountain be blessed: and rejoice with the wife of thy youth. . . .
> let her breasts satisfy thee at all times; and be thou ravished always with her love.[176]

---

175. Moses 5:1, 4.
176. Proverbs 5:18–19.

CHAPTER 9

THOU SHALT NOT COVET
ANOTHER'S ROLE

My mother died when I was in my thirties—long before I had come to appreciate her, her role, and how devotedly she filled it. In a moment of introspection one day, I told my children that I missed my mother. I told them that I wanted her to know that I've grown up. I wanted her to know that I know now how hard it was. I told my children that I wished I could sit down with her and tell her, "Mama, I understand now. I know how hard it is to be a woman. Your kind of woman."

My son was immediately defensive. "Are you telling me that you think it is harder to be a woman than it is to be a man?" (He does, after all, live in a world that has issues with this stuff.)

I thought about it and then answered slowly, "No, not really. But if we try to live our role as the family proclamation describes it—well, it is a different kind of hard. It requires a different kind of submission."

"How so?" The defensiveness had not dissipated. I continued.

"For one thing, look at the education process. A woman must choose a field to study just like a man must, but if she gets the ideal—according to the proclamation—she will not use her training in the workplace. It will enrich her life and her mothering, to be sure, but not her pocketbook or her reputation. The expanding expertise that she has been educated to want won't happen with what she is being told is the ideal. For many women, it makes it hard to buy into that definition of 'ideal.' It's a bit disconcerting to have so much of your energy given to something put into a "just in case" agenda. A woman may tell herself that she is completely faithful at the same time that she is bifurcated in her desire. Our natural man wants to have control in our world. It's hard for a natural woman to feel that she has the control she craves if she believes that she feels forced into her circumstance. She feels it unfair that she should have to choose between alternatives. She wants to be a mother in Israel but doesn't want to give up on that other thing she has prepared for. Society tells her she can have it all, and that's what she wants. She doesn't want to choose between them. She wants them both. Talk about opposing enticements, eh, Brother Lehi?[177] Then, of course, add to that the reality that when you get right down to it, only a small percentage gets the ideal of having a male provider for all of their lives anyway. We do live in a fallen world, remember."

My young son countered, "But the burden on the man to achieve that expanding expertise so that he can be the provider the proclamation requires—well, that's no picnic." I was quick to agree but was equally quick to point out that a nurturing, behind-the-scenes wife can be there to comfort and support him. My mind was still full of my own mother, who, after putting her many children to bed every night, helped my father take correspondence courses that furthered his earning capability. English was not his native tongue, and my mother's help was necessary.

"Not all women do that, Mom."

I knew that. "I guess we're back to ideals, aren't we?"

I loved the thought of my dear mother being an ideal. My son, in his wisdom, was contemplative. "Maybe the whole root of ideal is founded in both the man and the woman valuing and supporting both roles as the Lord has designed them."

All I could answer was, "Oh, yes!"

In my heart, I felt a spiritual witness that rarely is such a simple and profound solution offered to such a pervasive problem. I rolled it over again in my mind. *Maybe the whole root of ideal is founded in both the man and the woman valuing and supporting both roles as the Lord has designed them.* If that solution is as simple and profound as I think it is, then why do so few want to accept it? I think I know at least one of the reasons.

It gets back to that issue of control. It is an issue of vital importance to understand and for that reason has a chapter of its own. It is my belief that until—and unless—the definition of control (together with issues of agency) is understood, men and women will covet one another's roles.

---

177. 2 Nephi 2:11.

Both will believe that the other has it easier. Men will believe it must be wonderful not to have to punch a clock or be piled on by an employer. Women will believe that it must be glamorous to have the association of adults and to have business lunches. At church, men will believe it must be nice to just go home and not have endless meetings. Women will think it discriminatory that they don't have the priesthood.

What a great gift mutual understanding would be. A man needs to know in his heart, for instance, how difficult it is for a woman to have so much determined by her husband's job. She may have little input as to where they live, what hours they are free, what their social echelon is, and how much money they have to spend on needs and wants. Feeling that one is required to forfeit control over one's life can lead to some women suffering self-focus. Such feelings are of the wrong kind of nothingness. It is a problem not much different from that of someone with a lack of agency. That is why God the Father knew that only a plan of salvation that included agency would work. If only those women could see the choices they are making and the role of sacrifice in love. For other women, the fact of leading a life determined by their husband's work can lead to resentment. That is particularly true if their own training would allow for removing some of those limitations. The world tells us to trade places. Once again, having an accurate view of the plan of salvation and the role of each of us in it would help.

A man, on the other hand, might like to change jobs for one that pays less, or devote himself completely to one that pays more but takes him away from home responsibilities. Or maybe he would like to hitchhike around the world. Many men might laugh out loud at the thought that they are "in control."

A lot of the war between the sexes stems from a misunderstanding of our purpose here, how it is accomplished by becoming one flesh, and what it means to be in charge. Our natural men and women stupidly covet one another's roles. Society's way of dealing with that coveting is to eliminate the differences in the roles. The result has been to have both roles fail in many homes; therefore, "the one" they have become is lessened in substance. The way we should be dealing with it is for both of us to lovingly trust in the Lord's definition of our missions in the plan of salvation—live them in joyful devotion (no matter how good we are at them), even (or maybe especially) if it requires sacrifice—and reap the promised blessings. Those who choose that route, that trusting route, will know a joy that others will never know. They will be living the list. They will be kind and temperate, humble and diligent. They will not be seeking their own or vaunting themselves. As a result, they will eternally know Christ, which is the love we were sent here to know.[178]

To know Christ is to have eternal life. We take His name upon us and make our best effort to live by the attributes that are identified as His righteousness (the list). President Dallin H. Oaks has pointed out that as we take His name upon us, we should be aware that the word "name" should be treated as synonyms with His work and His plan.[179] The joy that man was created to feel was to take His name upon us, or, in other words, take His work for the plan of salvation upon us, thereby, to feel the pure love of Christ. He, in a wisdom that enormously exceeds our own, gives us roles and missions to help us on our way toward the understanding that comes from developing a critical mass of love.

That joyful state requires not just the acceptance of our roles, but also embracing them. We can trust that we will be able to do whatever He has asked with the developable resources He has provided. The fact that men are ordained to the priesthood and that women are blessed by the men who are given the priesthood is a central part of the Lord's design of our roles. Each of us is given what is necessary to best fill the role we have been given. Men need authority to do the ministering and administrative tasks that their role entails. Woman's role is, on the other hand, better benefited by partnership with the priesthood holders and being served by them. Men are ordained to be better able to serve us. That service enhances oneness in our relationships. It's a beautiful partnership design. Each brings to a unit those things that the other cannot bring.

It is my personal belief that a woman's influence in the world is more desirable than the administrative role is. But whatever role the Lord gives us is the role that we need to value. The roles that our Father in Heaven has in mind for us in the plan of salvation have been defined and made possible for us.[180] Let us love and trust God enough that we will not object to those roles. A list-living woman will not object to the authority

---

178. 2 Peter 1; 1 Corinthians 13; D&C 4; Alma 7.
179. Oaks, *His Holy Name,* chapter 4.
180. Among many other sources containing these definitions are Genesis 1:28 and "The Family: A Proclamation to the World."

men need to play their role. They will, instead, be grateful for priesthood service in their own roles.

The irony is that the primary resource that all of us have is the living of the list. A man's power does not come only from the enabling ordinance of receiving priesthood authority.

Doctrine and Covenants section 121 makes it clear that the power to keep that authority comes from living "the principles of righteousness."

> That the rights of the priesthood are inseparably connected with the powers of heaven, and that the powers of heaven cannot be controlled nor handled only upon the principles of righteousness.
>
> That they may be conferred upon us, it is true; but when we undertake to cover our sins or to gratify our pride, our vain ambition, or to exercise control or dominion or compulsion upon the souls of the children of men, in any degree of unrighteousness, behold, the heavens withdraw themselves; the Spirit of the Lord is grieved; and when it is withdrawn, Amen to that priesthood or the authority of that man.[181]

We who are given the opportunity to know Christ can seize it with all of our desire. We seize it with an effort to live the list. That is the only way, for men and women.

We take the name of Christ upon us and make our best effort to live by attributes that are defined as "His righteousness."

Interestingly, when the principles of righteousness are listed, they are neither gender specific nor calling limited. All of us, men and women, lowly and great, must get our power from living those principles. There is no differentiation in who can "know the Lord Jesus Christ" other than those who live for it will come to know and love Him, and those who don't won't.[182]

Both men's authority and women's influence depend upon such things as patience, long-suffering, kindness, and love unfeigned. The power for both a woman's influence and a man's ordained authority comes from righteousness. In other words, living the list.

The source of power to fill the roles given us, universally found in the same principles, makes it clear that coveting one another's roles is either an ignorance of or a rejection of those principles. We need not covet

---

181. D&C 121:36–37.
182. 2 Peter 1:7.

power, because we all have it. Men also need authority. They are given it. Only our roles are different.

In some cases (the temple for instance) where women's assigned duties require authority, they, too, are given it.

When the principles that make priesthood power possible are lacking, the priesthood power is shut off, and those same principles make a woman's power (or nurturing) possible or shut it off when they are lacking.

Women can be queens and priestesses, but only through that same power that makes a man's priesthood efficacious. Through that power, which is virtue and charity, we can gain confidence.[183]

The revelations will be "in their time,"[184] but the learning will be joyful.

I feel it is important to restate here what I consider obvious. Perfection is not of this world. Our power will therefore always be incomplete in this life. Our efforts can be given a fulness by the righteousness of our Savior. Even in the absence of our efforts, the Lord is able to circumvent our barriers when it is expedient in Him. That, however, is something we must not rely on. It is incumbent upon us to do all that we can to achieve a critical mass of righteous powerful love through our efforts and through our faith in the Lord Jesus Christ.

As Lehi told Jacob, "Wherefore, I know that thou art redeemed, because of the righteousness of thy Redeemer."[185]

Our great hope is always that some day our own righteousness will be all that is needed to develop a critical mass of love. As we deal here with true doctrine, we must remember that the joy of further light and knowledge must come in the Lord's way and time. It will be line upon line, precept upon precept[186] and must come through putting faith in the Lord Jesus Christ first. That faith, as Paul told us, is grounded in love for Him,[187] and it does not seek her own.

---

183. See D&C 121:45.
184. D&C5 9:4–5.
185. 2 Nephi 2:3.
186. 2 Nephi 28:30.
187. Ephesians 3:17.

According as his divine power hath given unto us all things that pertain unto life and godliness, through the knowledge of him that hast called us to glory and virtue. . . .

For if these things be in you and abound, they make you that ye shall neither be barren nor unfruitful in the knowledge of our Lord Jesus Christ.

But he that lacketh these things is blind, and cannot see afar off.[188]

Maybe the whole root of ideal is founded in both the man and the woman valuing and supporting both roles as the Lord has designed them.

---

188. 2 Peter 1:3, 8–9.

CHAPTER 10

THE POWER OF CONTROL VS. THE POWER OF INFLUENCE

A friend told me about a bumper sticker she saw recently: "A Woman's place is in control." We laughed, and then got serious. The bumper sticker represented something in our society that really isn't very funny.

This whole control issue needs more understanding than we have. Everybody wants control, no one thinks they have control, and we try all sorts of uglinesses to get control. Maybe if we just get angry enough, be unkind or demanding enough. Maybe we could pretend to be kind and instead manipulate. Maybe passive aggression will satisfy our need to be in charge. Maybe escape is the answer. If we can't control our circumstance, maybe we need to run to a circumstance that we *can* control. We put a lot of effort into getting control of our life and the lives of others.

Well, the joke's on us! As far as the important things are concerned, we do have control. We've always had it. It's called agency. No matter how others may try to limit our choices to their liking, who and what we are inside is up to us. They cannot go there. They cannot determine how we use the Light of Christ. In this life, there will be many situations where we are limited, but the antidote is rarely for us to find a way to seize control of the situation ourselves. The antidote is for us to remember that we are in control of our heart and mind. The unrighteous dominion of others should not be met by our own unrighteousness.

Much of our frustration in life comes from our desire to control the uncontrollable. The fallen world, by its very nature, usually isn't what we want it to be. All of us wish otherwise. Nevertheless, the only way we can deal with it is to recognize the self-control that is available through the Spirit and the Atonement of Christ.

There is great power in submission to inconsequential circumstance. Of course, our judgment as to what makes it inconsequential is all-important. Everything is, and should be, secondary to our ability to do what our Father in Heaven has given us to do. Inconvenience, pain, and even sorrow are worth submitting to if they make it possible for us to do the will of the Lord.[189]

I think of Joseph in Egypt submitting to slavery and then prison. Look at the power he accumulated there by knowing that he had control over his righteous self.[190] I think of his descendant Alma submitting to the wicked priests of Noah until the Lord gave the power to him and his followers to escape and do a great work.[191] I think of Christ, the ultimate in submissiveness, and the ultimate in His Father's power. [192]

As Doctrine and Covenants section 121 makes clear, the only everlasting dominion will always be without compulsory means.[193]

And yet, we want, seek, and sin to get control of those things that don't matter and that are accompanied by very little real power. A great many of the circumstances we must endure in order to do what the Lord would have us do really are inconsequential. We spend a lot of ourselves on "that which has no worth."[194]

I don't like to call it power when I think of what our desire for control can yield. It is, after all, the kind of power Satan pressed for in the war in heaven and the kind of power that will require much healing by the Atonement of Christ. I suppose it can be called power, however, since such an intense desire for control is so destructive. But when compared to the power of love, submission, and influence, the power of control is so puny and temporary. Foolishly, it is often the power people focus on. Particularly women. Truly and paradoxically, speaking for myself, there is no time I feel more powerless than when I am focusing on my desire to control.

---

189. See Mosiah 3:19.
190. Genesis 39–40.
191. Mosiah 17–18.
192. Luke 23:34; Luke 22:42.
193. D&C 121:46.
194. 2 Nephi 9:51.

I've always thought of the power of a woman in the home as being that greater power, or the power of love. There is little virtue in a focus on herself, her control, or her lack of control. She is in a position to have what is the greatest power we mortals can have: influence.

A mother has the power to influence generations of God's children. I grant that only happens when her desire is great enough to sacrifice for it; maybe even submit to less than lovely material circumstances for it. But if she takes the opportunity, she is practicing godliness and is in possession of power indeed.

I love what Walt Whitman said in "Song of Myself." He wrote, "I am not a mother. I am the mother of those who will be mothers in their time."[195]

He is using motherhood as an absolute metaphor for the influence and importance he is hoping to achieve with his writing.

It is an understanding that President Russell M. Nelson had when he said, "The deep longing of my heart to make a difference in the world—like only a mother does—bubbled up from my heart. Through the years, whenever I have been asked why I chose to become a medical doctor, my answer has always been the same: 'Because I could not choose to be a mother.'"[196]

Many parents, both mothers and fathers, believe that control will raise children with a desire to be faithful: no television, a strict schedule, etc. Order is good, but by itself, such discipline may have limited value. Such things may accompany love, but they are not a substitute for love. The presence of excessive rules and checklists will not cause our children to want to follow our example and give us dominion. The presence of godliness in the home will. It is living God's list of loving attributes that creates influence.[197] "Charity never faileth."[198]

In the process of loving, parents become more than they otherwise would become, and in the process of that becoming, their children—generations of their children—will give them everlasting dominion without compulsory means. Such is the plan, but the family opportunity

---

195. Walt Whitman, "Songs of Myself," *Leaves of Grass* (Poetry Foundation, 1892).

196. Russell M. Nelson, "Sisters' Participation in the Gathering of Israel," *Ensign*, Nov. 2018.

197. D&C 121:41, 46.

198. 1 Corinthians 13:8.

must be given priority. Like all facets of eternal life, if we don't want those blessings, we can say no thank you.

Men and women both know (even if only subliminally) that ultimately positive and creative power is what our Father in Heaven has in mind to give us.[199] We have only glimpses of it in this life, but when we have those peeks, they are overwhelmingly beautiful. Satan is only too happy to suggest control as a shortcut to that power, but it ends up creating behavior that must ultimately be overcome by the power of a loving Atonement. How foolish we are. How foolish mankind has always been in that regard.

Control cannot bring everlasting dominion. Dominion that will flow unto us forever and ever must be without compulsory means. Control, beyond the conditioning of childhood, is absolutely antithetical to influence.

Focusing on the love we have for others to the point of sacrificing for them results in influence that leads to that great power. That sacrifice often requires ignoring less-desirable circumstances and just loving those we are serving. Often we must sacrifice an ideal circumstance to achieve an ideal love. And love is where power comes from, not circumstance. The paradox is, that in sharing that love, control over our circumstance may ensue. But it is not determinative of our power. It is a by-product of it.

When we choose to love—and make no mistake, love is a choice—peace with our choices is the manifestation of our self-control. That is the power and glory God wants us to have. That is the purpose of this fallen world and is the reason we chose to come to it. The entire plan of salvation is based on whether or not we choose to love and to sacrifice for that love. For the plan to work, our world can in no way be controlled for our ease. Not by us. Not by our loving Father in Heaven. No matter that Satan continues to tell us that it can be controlled and self-indulgent. The Lord prepares a table for us in the *presence* of our enemies. That table is the comfort of His shepherding through the uncontrolled circumstance around us.[200] We will feel the power of walking beside the still waters only when we understand that.

---

199. Moses 1:39.
200. Psalms 23.

Our righteous choices will allow us to create order in our worlds and enable us to feel the security of living in the world without being of it.[201] But the world itself will remain unpredictable and often harsh.

Still, our wise Creator has given us control over our inner core. Only we can control how our circumstance will affect us. If we are filled with the love of Christ and for one another, we can have the peace of our self-control.

A friend asked me, "What about, say, a person loses their job. The world is going to virtually collapse for them. Their employer has control over the well-being of that inner core you're talking about."

My answer was, "No, he doesn't. He has control over their comfort and their material resources for a period. He may even have the ability to cause tears and anxiety. But he does not have the ability to choose who you are inside—only the torment you must go through. He may be able to choose your discomfort all right, but it is your own choice whether you will allow him to change your faith, your determination, or your trajectory. All of that is in your power, not his. Our earthly happiness and our eternal joy require us to keep that perspective about power. Interestingly, I have seen men in this position and found it fascinating that they tend to try harder during periods like that to exert control over their wives and family. It can't really work, but it tends to be the response to what they are going through."

The problem such a man might have is not unique. When one's craving for control overwhelms one, he or she tries to enforce an impossible control over others as a substitute for the self-control. Of all the fantasies, that can be the most damaging, because control is contraindicated by, and an anathema to, the love that can sustain one in one's efforts at that inner core strength.

Dr. Viktor Frankl (a psychiatrist) wrote a wonderful book called *Man's Search for Meaning.*[202] He was a Jewish prisoner in a Nazi concentration camp, and his whole thesis of the book is that no matter what happened in the camp (and the tale is grim) no one else could control his mind and heart, and therefore, no one could control him. That knowledge not only made it possible for him to psychologically survive, but it also gave him the strength to help others.

---

201. See Romans 12:2.
202. Viktor Frankl, *Man's Search for Meaning* (Boston, MA: Beacon Press, 1959).

When we choose to sacrifice the small pearls of our life in order to buy the pearl of great price, it will not stop us from feeling pain and suffering sometimes. The question—asked by the Lord and answered by us, is whether we will give up our agency and/or our circumstance to worldly controllers or whether we will keep them for ourselves. If we keep them for ourselves, what will we do with them? Will we give the power over our well-being to the love of our Father in Heaven? Who we give the power to is key. All power over us is a gift to whomever we "list to obey."[203]

Feeling peace in our own role instead of coveting the role of another requires that understanding of power. If we lack it, we will feel put upon and miserable a lot of the time. 'Twas ever thus. One huge barrier to getting there is believing that we have no control at all—that we have no choice at all. We hear it every day: "I had no choice. I had to_____" (fill in the blank). That statement denies the entire plan of salvation. Not to mention that it is never true.

In another book,[204] I told the story of a woman—a physician—who made the mistake of believing she had no choice. Especially since the story is about motherhood, I decided to include it here:

I heard a doctor speak of her limitations with the declaration that she had no choice. One of her children had emotional problems that the psychiatrist said could only be cared for by having his mother at home. Her response was that she would have liked to continue to practice medicine but that she had no choice. Of course she had a choice. She could have ignored her child's mental health and practiced medicine instead. That alternative was certainly available. To her credit, that option was too horrific to consider, but she could have chosen it.

Her well-being would have been so much better served had she seen it as a choice she wanted to make. It would have made it possible for her to feel the power of her agency. Seeing it as a decision would have given her awareness that her love for her child was worth more to her than anything else. Perhaps most important, she would have avoided the certain melancholy of feeling the victim in the matter. The knowledge that we are choosing gives us all those happy advantages. Moroni often talked of the danger of denying the gift and power of God. This mother, by denying her agency, was denying a great gift from God that would have made

---

203. Mosiah 2:32.
204. Ester Rasband, *That I May Behold* (Highland UT: Rasband Books, 2015).

her more powerful, more loving, and happier. There would have been no feelings of victimization had she been grateful that it was within her power to choose to give her child a healthy future.

Just because we cannot choose reality or choose two things at once doesn't mean we are left without power. Just because we don't get to choose the alternatives does not mean that we cannot choose between them. It is vitally important that we acknowledge that the choice between right and wrong—especially in our roles—is always ours and is always powerful.

The same friend who talked about the job loss asked me this:

"But the Lord honors our agency so much that He would never circumscribe our choices. He would welcome us on the path without requiring our choices change. Right?"

"I'm afraid," I said, "that you have a wrong view of the character of God. And therefore of agency. I guess now I see why Joseph Smith said a correct view of God's character will be essential to save us.[205] You think agency means a broad path. He speaks of a narrow path. We hear so often, "I'm sure God understands." I'm sure of it too. That is why He prepared other kingdoms of glory for those who just didn't want His path enough to choose it. The paths we choose, because of His understanding, may still lead to glory, but just not celestial glory. We have complete freedom to choose whether or not to be on His path. But we don't get to choose to broaden it. No one comes on that path without choosing His way. It's highly circumscribed, for sure, but the paradox is that the self-control that leads to peaceful power within us is a major portion of the ability to put aside seeking one's own. Humble losing of self is foundational to the critical mass of the Lord's kind of love. As we read in *Lectures on Faith*, lecture six:

> It is in vain for persons to fancy to themselves that they are heirs with those, or can be heirs with them, who've offered their all in sacrifice.

The understanding that we must have in order to be eternally happy, to make the choice to do things the Lord's way, is often called too restrictive or unfair. But here's the truth of it. There is only one way to become children of Christ and therefore part of the eternal family of our Father in Heaven. All roads may lead to Rome, but not to the Holy Spirit of

---

205. Smith, *Lectures on Faith*, 3.

Promise. We need to know what we must do to get on the "way." So He gives it to us. We have scripture, prophets, and the Holy Ghost. It certainly isn't too restrictive or unfair for us to have that information. He tells us how to get there if we want to go. If we don't want to go, we simply don't follow those instructions. He is committed to giving us the right to say, "No, thank you." We cannot say we don't have a choice. The choice is clear. Unfortunately, we think the very act of having to choose is restrictive and unfair. We want to get to God on our own path instead of His. It won't work. Only one path will get us there. It's a behavioral path—a list living path. We are well informed about it. If we want to follow it, we can. If we want to avoid it, we can. If we have strayed off of it and want to get back to it, through the Atonement of Christ, we can. It's our choice.

I should mention here what my grandson recently reminded me. There are, in mortality, some for whom choice is not possible. There may be mental illness, for instance. There may be abuse that renders them spiritually disabled. I have long felt that there even could be children raised in a Latter-day Saint home where there has not been an example of the joy of living the gospel. That joyless home can leave those children unable to see the Lord's path as a joyful choice. Under any of those circumstances, perhaps the ultimate judge may consider these folks unable to find or choose the Lord's path. Only God knows our hearts, and only He knows whether we have had the chance to choose. We do need to remember that the decision as to whether we had a fair chance to choose here in mortality is God's to make, not ours. His judgment that we had no chance here does not mean that we can be exalted without making the choice. Choice remains the only way. Therefore, our Father in Heaven will still ultimately give the opportunity to choose to all. Their opportunity and responsibility will still be to examine the enticings and make the choice. It's part of the plan for all to do so. With light and with experience, that choice will be made available. God will force no man to celestialization. That fact *must* be acknowledged if the comfort of His love is to be felt.

And that comfort, brothers and sisters, is what makes everything worth it—the difficulties of our own roles and missions, that giving up of coveting the roles of others, the pain that others can put us through—

everything. Oh, how I want that pearl of great price, that pearl of love and joy—all the way to critical mass.

> Beloved, let us love one another: for love is of God; and every one that loveth is born of God, and knoweth God.[206]

---

206. 1 John 4:7.

Part 3

The Fulness of Joy Potential

If by the grace of God ye are perfect in Christ,
ye can in nowise deny the power of God.

—Moroni 10:32

CHAPTER 11

SONS OF ADAM AND DAUGHTERS OF EVE

*I*n earlier chapters, we talked of Adam and Eve in the Garden. It's entirely appropriate, because we can and must identify ourselves as sons of Adam and daughters of Eve. I often think about that identification when things get tough. Mother Eve certainly had no bed of roses in her assignment to begin this population. She and Adam were the ultimate pioneers, with all the hard work that implies. They worked together in the field.[207] They prayed together and heard the answers together.[208] Although their emotions are not recorded for us, I'm sure they suffered anguish together. Most of their children "loved Satan more than God,"[209] and one of their sons murdered his brother. This hard life lasted for several hundred years. Every time I think about Eve it is with enormous admiration and no small amount of pain in my empathy. I can only imagine that a man might feel the same when he seeks to emulate Adam. There is great gain in us seeking to emulate those first parents.

With a life of great sacrifice, Adam and Eve willingly made it possible for us to come to this world and have an opportunity to make our own choices. Their role in life and their partnership is well worth our focus.

Unfortunately, the focus on Eve is almost always on what she knew or did not know before *her* choice was made. It's almost an intellectual

---

207. Moses 5:1.
208. Moses 5:4.
209. Moses 5:13.

parlor game to talk about whether or not there was another way, whether or not she knew that the fall was necessary.

The truth is, we, too—both sons of Adam and daughters of Eve—made a choice to come to this fallen world.[210] We, too, made that choice in order to take our part in the plan of salvation. We, too, accepted the role to make opportunities for others to choose. We, too, made the commitment to bear and/or influence future generations. It seems to me, therefore, that the most helpful focus we can have on Eve and Adam is what they did with their choice—not what they knew before they made it. And it was *their* choice. The entrance into the fallen world was like a check that needs two signatures. They both signed. That is the example of what we can do with *our* two signature checks. Husbands and wives must make commitments together and stand behind them together.

What Eve knew before her choice doesn't really matter to us. For both Adam and Eve, their choice was made. It was made to fill their roles on earth, and so was ours. Knowing how they stood behind their decision, and knowing what they did after the choice was made—now that's helpful.

Examining their behavior, one thing we know is that Eve and Adam knew they needed to stay together to fill their roles in the plan of salvation. My feeling is that "staying together" meant more than just geographically. They knew what it meant to be one. They both knew that leaving their cushy Garden circumstance was necessary to do that. They both humbly knew that they needed further light and knowledge to fill those roles. They both were willing to obey and to make covenants with their Father in Heaven. We can follow those examples.

We don't know a lot about their marriage—just a few things from Genesis and a few more from Moses chapters 5 and 6 (and some conjecture from Mark Twain). It is clear, though, that they worked together and worshipped together. We have absolutely no scriptural evidence that there was any separateness in their relationship.

We know that Adam named Eve.[211] He gave her the name of Eve because she was to be "the mother of all living." To me, this naming showed Adam's understanding of the importance of his wife's decision. It

---

210. "Jesus Christ, Our Chosen Leader and Savior," chapter 3, *Gospel Principles* (Salt Lake City: The Church of Jesus Christ of Latter-day Saints, 2009).
211. Moses 4:26.

also showed his honor and respect for what that self-sacrificing decision meant."[212] The heavy-duty commitment was worthy of that honoring. In my view, it was a choice that had to be made first with the agency of woman, because Eve and her daughters would bear the children. However, as Eliza R. Snow wrote, parents are not single in heaven.[213] Adam validated Eve's decision with equal devotion so that the family of man might have a beginning.

The name that meant "the mother of all living" had an additional value for Eve. Her very given name kept her in remembrance of that role.

Eve was not the only name that our first mother was given. God Himself gave to her and her husband a shared name. "He called *their name* Adam."[214] I see God's name-giving and their sharing of that name as being an important symbol of God's intent that the two of them should become one: "Bone of my bone, flesh of my flesh."[215] When Eve was formed from the cells of Adam's rib, it is clear to me that absolute connection with one another was the goal our Father in Heaven had in mind for us. It takes time and work to become so completely "one," but step by step, it can happen. And *God gave* couples the same name as one another to put us in remembrance of our roles and missions. It is the most important goal we can take upon us in this life. No wonder marriages that reach fifty years are called golden and the symbol at sixty years is the diamond.

Prophets have told us that God is a part of our marriage covenant.[216] That is because He is the one who has given us the commandment to have the same name, the same goals, and a totally shared future. That is the reminder that having the same name is supposed to give us.

That is as true as the opposite that is taking place in our world. To not have the same name is a reminder that we are separate—and what's more, we are not taking those steps to be one. Women who marry and decide to continue to be known by their father's name are trying to make a statement. Keeping their maiden name is a stated symbol that they

---

212. Genesis 3:20.
213. "O My Father," *Hymns*, no. 292, third verse.
214. Genesis 5:2; see Moses 6:9.
215. Moses 3:23.
216. See Ezra Taft Benson, "Marriage and Family—Ordained of God," chapter 14, *Teachings of the Presidents of the Church* (Salt Lake City: The Church of Jesus Christ of Latter-day Saints, 2014).

want to have an independent identity from their husband. I struggle to understand this. It seems as if they feel threatened by the "one flesh" stepping-stone to exaltation. And it *is* a stepping-stone to exaltation. As section 132, verse 7, of the Doctrine and Covenants reminds us:

> For these angels did not abide my law; therefore, they cannot be enlarged, but remain separately and singly, without exaltation, in their saved condition, to all eternity; and from henceforth are not gods, but are angels of God forever and ever.

It would seem clear that the choice to be individually separate here on earth is a choice to be separate in the next life as well. We must remember that the whole purpose of coming to this fallen world is to make the behavioral decision as to how much glory we will reach toward. If we don't want to be exalted, we don't have to be. We simply show our Father in Heaven that we want less than that. Remember President Russell M. Nelson's words that salvation is individual but exaltation is a family matter. A family with a shared name; a family formed by a "one flesh" couple.

President Dallin H. Oaks has written that when we take the name of the Savior upon us, it means to take His work and His plan upon us—and ultimately, His essence.[217] It is not a haphazard metaphor when the scriptures call Christ the "bridegroom" and His covenant people the "bride." When we marry, we women take our husband's name upon us. It means the same as the name-taking between each of us and our Savior. It means taking upon us our husband's work and his plans. We not only present a profound partnership influence on our husband's plans and his work, but we also bring our unique gifts and talents to complement his. Consecrated giving is the same exercise we experience when we bring all our gifts to the altar as we take on the mission of our Savior in the plan of salvation. In that chain of joinings, our gifts are ironically honed, not abandoned. Devoted love is a powerful sharpener. I can certainly bear testimony to Nephi's truth that charity is love, and without charity, we are nothing.

It is certainly less than easy to understand that submission brings triumph, that losing self makes possible the finding of self, that abasement is required for exaltation, and that putting others first leads to confidence and an everlasting dominion without compulsory means. All these things are true. Paradox is almost always the Lord's way.

---

217. Oaks, *His Holy Name*, chapter 4.

It's important to note that sacrifice is the name of the game for both men and women. There is a great obligation of partnership that attaches to him who *gives* his name to another. It is a pattern of name giving and taking. As the restored gospel teaches, those who desired that the Savior should put His name upon them: they would receive all that He had to give.[218] The same is true when a man gives his name to his wife. He bestows all his worldly goods and his eternal fidelity on her and shares with her an eternal inheritance. Once the name is given and taken, it can only be blotted out by transgression.[219] When a husband gives his name and his wife takes it, that is exactly the sacred security that we give one another. It is the most powerful of mortal partnerships. Both must approach it with list-living commitment. When the commitment is absent (and we have all witnessed marriages where that commitment is absent), well, that lack is indeed transgression and blots out the name taking and giving. The joining chain of man, woman, and God, is then missing a link. If there are righteous links in the chain remaining, they are still linked to the Master, and their eternal life is in His all-wise hands.

Righteous women take a husband's name upon them with the hope and intent of eternal fidelity. Righteous husbands give their names with the same hope and intent, because their goal is to be one with one another in essence. That means their individual goals are now "our" goals and their individual identities "ours" as well. In an exalted world, we will have to be one with one another in order to also be one with our Father in Heaven and His Son Jesus Christ. The opposite is also true. Because being one flesh is required, if we work to stay separate, we are working to stay separate from God. Therefore, enduring in the righteousness of complete commitment and selfless identification is essential. I suppose that is why the Lord said "few there be that find it."[220] But the good news is that the deeper we can make our love and integrity become, the more support we both have to try to live the Lord's way.

Many women try to explain their reluctance to name taking with such statements as "I feel like I'm losing my identity." The Savior addressed this issue long ago: "Lose yourself for my sake to find yourself."[221] We also hear "I have to find myself first—then I can give." To that one,

---

218. D&C 84:35–38.
219. Mosiah 5:11.
220. Matthew 7:14.
221. Matthew 16:25.

the Savior pre-answered: "Seek ye first the kingdom of God and his righ-teousness and all else shall be added unto you."[222] Another familiar state-ment: "If I get absorbed in my husband, then who am I?" The Lord's pre-answer, in the words of King Benjamin are,

> And now, because of the covenant which ye have made ye shall be called the children of Christ, his sons, and his daughters; for behold, this day he hath spiritually begotten you; for ye say that your hearts are changed through faith on his name; therefore, ye are born of him and have become his sons and his daughters.[223]

It turns out that name taking is not just basic to the gospel. It *is* the gospel. It is no wonder that the adversary would use everything in his bag of tricks to discourage us from understanding its importance. There are entire cultures where the diffusion of what Adam and Eve understood is distorted and/or has been absent for millennia. The whole "good news" is that we can, through sacrificial choice, become one with our mate, one with our Savior, and therefore one with the Father of us all, for which identification we can receive everything the Father has. To take on the work and the plan of Christ is humbling. Of course it is. That's the whole point. We cannot be exalted without abasing our-selves.[224] Giving up other identification of self, such as our own past surname, is a symbol of that humility and the extent of that desire to be one with Him. The desire needs to be complete. Like King Lamoni's father, we need to be willing to give not just half of our kingdom, but all that He requires. Our sins. Our kingdom. All of it,[225] just as He has prioritized it. It's called consecration. That completeness, that wholeness, is represented by name taking. That is what makes it possible to actu-ally become "children of Christ," inheritors of the Father, and kings and queens. It is the "Christian paradox," which Elder Maxwell frequently spoke about.[226] And so, completing the paradox, by being willing to give and take in our marriages, we all end up having the name of Christ be

---

222. Matthew 6:33.
223. Mosiah 5:7.
224. D&C 112:3; 2 Corinthians 11:7; Matthew 23:12; D&C 124:14; Luke 18:14; D&C 101:42; Luke 14:11.
225. Alma 22:15.
226. Neal A. Maxwell, "Settle This in Your Hearts," *Ensign*, Nov. 1992.

the "name by which [we will be] called."[227] This includes both men and women. We get the ultimate name and all of its blessings only if we are not clinging to another name.

It seems counter intuitive to seek infinite and eternal greatness with absolute and abject abasement. But that necessary paradox is what Eve found and learned about the fall.

We speak so much of being free. The irony is that freedom only comes from submitting to the paradox.

> And under this head ye are made free, and there is no other head whereby ye can be made free. There is no other name given whereby salvation cometh; therefore, I would that ye should take upon you the name of Christ, all you that have entered into the covenant with God that ye should be obedient unto the end of your lives.
>
> And it shall come to pass that whosoever doeth this shall be found at the right hand of God, for he shall know the name by which he is called; for he shall be called by the name of Christ.[228]

Of course, this ultimate eternal freedom to have creative joy and energy is preceded by the freedom to choose to seek it or not. The choice to have this glorious eternal blessing is made with behaviors: what James would call "the works" that give life to faith.[229]

When King Benjamin taught these things to his people, he acknowledged that some might choose not to pay the price of meaningful taking of the name of Christ. That reminds me again of the letter my brother sent when I became engaged: "And rest assured your Father in Heaven is watching. If you do not show him you like being a wife, he will not trouble you with that role in the eternities." Or as King Benjamin expressed it:

> And now it shall come to pass, that whosoever shall not take upon him the name of Christ must be called by some other name; therefore, he findeth himself on the left hand of God.[230]

---

227. Alma 5:38.
228. Mosiah 5:8–9.
229. James 2:20.
230. Mosiah 5:10.

Inasmuch as "Nevertheless neither is the man without the woman, neither the woman without the man, in the Lord,"[231] the effort for a man and woman to be one with one another is part and parcel of being one with God. When a woman takes her husband's name in marriage, they both show the willingness to leave off their separateness and become one. The sacrifices they make for each other show their willingness to take on the name of Christ.

I can't imagine a self worth guarding in mortality that would bring as much joy as finding oneself with God.

This leads me to something else that Eve knew. It is something that we, too, can know by following her example. While still in her mortal experience, Eve recorded that she knew the joy of her redemption.[232] She knew that it was worth everything she had been through. I'm sure that by living the list, the principles of righteousness, she kept her equilibrium her entire difficult life. She did not seek her own or vaunt herself. Had she a mind to focus on her own well-being, I don't think she would have taken on her significant mission. She and Adam were one flesh. They had used this life to "prepare to meet God."[233] They, I'm sure, are now abiding perfect love.

> The eternal importance of gender and of eternal marriage can be properly understood only within the context of our Heavenly Father's plan of happiness. Emphasizing the institution of marriage without linking it adequately to the simple and fundamental doctrine of the plan cannot provide sufficient direction, protection, and hope in a world confused about these vital issues.[234]

---

231. See 1 Corinthians 11:8–11.
232. Moses 5:11.
233. Alma 34:32.
234. David A. Bednar, *Increase in Learning* (Salt Lake City: Deseret Book, 2011), 154.

CHAPTER 12

JOY IN ONENESS:
THE CRITICAL MASS OF LOVE

*I*t was another one of those dinner parties. The man next to me said, "I understand you write books. Why?" He proceeded to give his own answer: "Of course, I know why. It's because your husband is a great man and you have had to live in the shadow of his accomplishments. So you decided to write books and get a little attention."

I answered, "My husband *is* a great man," and I intended to go on, but my husband interrupted. He said some kind things about me, including mentioning the support he feels I have been in his life. Then I went on: "Every book I have written has been because the two of us have been talking, an idea will surface, and my husband will say, 'That's a book!' Then he will—shall we call it encourage—me to get to it. He is so self-disciplined that it is hard for him to understand that I have to wait for the muse to hit, so he tries to create blocks of time for me. He does the research and endless editing. The books are not even something I do without him, let alone in competition with him."

My husband spoke again. "She made my contributions possible. I only hope I have helped her with hers." Mine or his, our achievements have been "ours."

I realize that telling this story is more than a little self-serving. I also know that negative examples teach more than positive ones do. Still, I include it. I warned in my introduction that this would be a testimony that family life the Lord's way works. Our companion at that dinner table represents exactly what the world has come to expect in a marriage: Competition. Resentment. How can it be anything else in a marriage of two people who are guarding against what they see as the danger of losing their individuality? When the self is something one believes should not be sacrificed, the result is anything but godly joy. On the other hand, the story also shows the love and grateful joy that comes when two people decide to be one. Make no mistake. It is a decision. When we try to be one, we're joyful. When we guard against being taken advantage of, or against having our "self" diminished, the very guarding sets us up for competition and resentment. Not to mention misery. It is all about the presence or the absence of "the list" in us.

Prophets throughout the ages have exhausted themselves trying to get us to understand how important the attributes of godliness are that lead to a decision of oneness. When we understand, we, too, want to teach that importance. Oh, that our families "might partake."[235]

I'm often drawn to the great minds of literature and philosophy who have discovered the value of coming together in unity. It is not unusual for great artists to be blessed with sacred understanding. "No man is an island," John Donne reminded us,[236] and yet we continue to maintain a sea of separateness around ourselves. "All are but parts of one stupendous whole," said Alexander Pope,[237] and our response is "Not me!" We work to keep ourselves separate without regard for the wisdom of people like Alexander Dumas: "All for one, one for all. That is our device."[238]

Listen to the words of Pierre Teillard de Chardin, who puts the principle into scientific reality:

> If there were no internal propensity to unite, even at a prodigiously rudimentary level—indeed, in the very molecule itself—it would be physically impossible for love to appear higher up. . . . Driven by the forces of love, the fragments of the world seek each other so that the world can come into being.[239]

All of these great minds are acknowledging their understanding that the pinnacle of human experience comes from being one with one

---

235. 1 Nephi 8:11–12.

236. From John Donne's *Devotions upon Emergent Occasions*, 1624.

237. Alexander Pope, "Essay on Man," *The Oxford Book of English Mystical Verse*; ed. D. H. S. Nicholson and A. H. E. Lee; contr. A. K. Clark (Oxford, United Kingdom: Oxford University Press, 1917), 52.

238. Alexander Dumas, *The Three Musketeers*, 1st ed. (Collinsville, MS: Heritage Press, 1950).

239. Rasband, *Man and Woman, Joy in Oneness*.

another, and therefore one with our God—a circumstance that cannot happen in the absence of "the principles of righteousness."

These insights, however, are merely testimonies to the beautiful and powerful clarity of the admonishments to oneness in the scriptures. Nowhere has it been expressed with such strength and poetry as it was by Paul when he said that man is nothing unless he has love, which never seeks its own interests.[240]

And nowhere has it been expressed with such beauty and love as when the Savior prayed, "Holy Father, keep through thine own name those whom thou hast given me, that they may be one, as we are."[241]

It is so deeply thrilling to know how dearly He wanted that joy for us. He showed us, taught us, and died for us that we might achieve that joy:

> Master, which is the great commandment in the law?
>
> Jesus said unto him, Thou shalt love the Lord thy God with all thy heart, and with all thy soul, and with all thy mind.
>
> This is the first and great commandment.
>
> And the second is like unto it, Thou shalt love thy neighbor as thyself.[242]

I have before referred to the careful guarding of the self as "treasuring our separateness."[243] If that is the treasure we seek, we can have it, but it is not the pure love of Christ. It cannot make it possible for Christ to exalt us.

Only the losing of self will help us find it, and that which we lose for others is losing ourselves "for his sake."[244]

It requires us to be full of Christ-defined love. Only then will we have the critical mass that will make it possible for us to experience perfect love forever. We must feel that loving unity in our families and in our world in general. That is the critical mass of love, and therefore, joy.

All of the scriptures exist to teach us that lesson. They give us positive and negative examples and positive and negative commandments. The

---

240. 1 Corinthians 13:2.
241. John 17:11.
242. Matthew 22:34–40.
243. Rasband, *Man and Woman, Joy in Oneness*, 2.
244. Matthew 16:25–26.

"thou shalt nots" are only stepping stones to the ultimate "thou shalts." All are but parts, as Pope would say, of one stupendous whole. And, as Christ would say: on which hang all the law and the prophets. That whole is love—the kind of love that leads to being one with God and with one another—each love like unto the other. Only when we can achieve a critical mass of that love and unity, that portion[245] of celestialization, can He perfect us with a grand and exponential growth to perfect love forever.

In a discussion recently, I made the comment that the scriptures were just a bunch of different men finding different ways to teach us to work at developing the attributes of perfect love.

"They are all about love and nothing else."

My friend said, "Well, love and repentance."

But isn't repentance just like obedience and feeding His sheep? Isn't it all about love? We repent and obey and serve because we love God enough to want to be with him. Otherwise, it is just self-help, and therefore not at all the real taking of His yoke upon us. Self-help works to improve us sometimes, but not permanently. Benjamin Franklin, whose autobiography is considered the first self-help book, tells of thirteen flaws in himself that he decided to work on.[246] He worked at them one at a time and found that by the time he got to the thirteenth, he was weak on what he had put as number one and had to go back and start over. So it is with changes in our life that "seek our own" or "vaunt ourselves."[247] Those changes can be rewarding, but there is an end to the benefit.

"Verily I say unto you, they have their reward." [248]

The promise is that when our love leads us to self-sacrificing choices in order to share the mission of Christ, He can indeed reveal himself to us and cause our critical mass of love and joy. Real repentance, like all real obedience, must be an act of love. And indeed, though we may call it repentance, without that motivation, we will never taste of the pure white fruit.[249]

Dostoevsky, a deeply devoted Russian Christian from the mid-nineteenth century wrote a masterpiece entitled *The Brothers Karamazov.*[250]

---

245. See D&C 88.
246. Benjamin Franklin, *Memoirs of Benjamin Franklin* (1791).
247. 1 Corinthians 13.
248. Matthew 6:5–6.
249. See 1 Nephi 11.
250. Fyodor Dostoevsky, *The Brothers Karamazov.* First published as a serial in *The Russian Messenger,* January 1879 to November 1880. Dostoevsky died less than four months after its publication.

In it, he captures the understanding of a life that changes to a motivation of love. Dostoevsky is deeply respectful of the redeeming power. Perhaps my favorite concept from the book is this: Hell is the inability to love. It will be what we want in the end, but will have spurned here—to our infinite regret.

Dostoevsky's plot is complex, but suffice it to say that in the end, Dmitri Karamazov cannot accept the offered escape from his punishment unless he gives his all to helping a child reconnect with his father. That is what we too must do. That is the condition God has given us. In order to reach the critical mass, we must reach to seize every opportunity to help our fellows reconnect with their Father in Heaven. That requires being nurturers in whatever role we are assigned. That is true for both men and women. All must nurture in order to know Christ.

If she is privileged to follow the ideal of the plan of salvation, a mother is blessed to be a full-time nurturer. We must seize our opportunity—undiluted by personal ambition. It is not just that it is the most important of our roles—and well worth the sacrifice of other activities—but if we purposefully reject it, we say "no, thank you" to the greatest of all gifts. Perfect celestial love is that gift we cannot receive unless, in this life, we achieve a portion—a critical mass. Far from being one of limits (as some see it), woman's role is designed by our Father in Heaven to be expansive. It is designed to help us develop all the important things: patience, long-suffering, and love unfeigned. It can make our soul swell within us.[251] It can leave us with empathy, wisdom, and understanding. In addition, it allows for the greatest productivity imaginable. We may have less visibility, but we leave a powerful legacy of missionary work and eternal influence. Limiting? No, I don't think so.

As Shakespeare has expressed it: "Who sells eternity to buy a toy?"[252]

This life is not about being seen of men. (Though that is certainly one of the enticings in a fallen world.) It is about developing enough of the attributes of perfect love[253] that Christ will be able to give us a fulness. That is the whole purpose of coming here. We exercise against opposition so that we can be strong in our humble commitment to take His yoke upon us. In the process, we become one flesh with our husbands,

---

251. See Alma 32.
252. William Shakespeare, "The Rape of Lucrece" (1594).
253. See D&C 107:30; 2 Peter 1; D&C 121.

and/or one with our fellow men. We must always remember (as quoted above) what Christ wanted for us when all was said and done:

> Holy Father, keep through thine own name those whom thou hast given me, that they may be one, as we are.[254]

> The desire to be one will put us on the path to it. And our desire comes out of our own sovereign heart.[255]

> It's called agency. It is called acting instead of being acted upon.[256]

If we get to live a life of full-time Christ-defined loving, why on earth would we say no thank you?

> Stand fast in [the] liberty wherewith ye have been made free [by Christ].[257]

> Choose you this day whom ye will serve.[258]

> I am woman.
> If there is pride in man there is pride in me,
> For I am part of him.
> I am his partner, his energy, his heart.
> If either of us treasures any separateness,
> Looks to the part and not the whole,
> The soul of all eternity is lost to us,
> For joy in oneness is the godlike role."

—Ester Rasband, frontispiece
Man and Woman, Joy in Oneness

---

254. John 17:11.
255. Maxwell, "The Tugs and Pulls of the World."
256. See 2 Nephi 2:16.
257. Mosiah 23:13.
258. Joshua 24:15.

CHAPTER 13

A GLIMPSE

*O*rdinarily, I'm uncomfortable at funerals. Hearing all the wonderful things about other people makes it hard for me to avoid self-focus. Shame on me, I know, but my own inadequacy takes center stage.

Recently, however, I attended a funeral that deeply inspired me. It was for a woman who had a large family and a larger posterity. The family had to reserve the entire center section of our large chapel and the first few rows of each side. All the talks focused on the fact that the most important thing to their mother/grandmother was that they all have testimonies of the gospel. The announcement was that there would follow a musical number called "Our testimony." I remembered a song with a similar name and expected to hear it.

What a surprise! Almost everyone in those reserved rows left their seats and went to the stand. A few scattered family members remained in their places. The overflowing group on the stand proceeded to bear their testimony to the remarkable woman. They sang, "I Know That My Redeemer Liveth" with the most powerful and meaningful tone I have ever heard. They bore the testimony that their dear mother/grandmother wanted them to have. The angels heard it, I'm sure.

One would have thought, considering my weakness, I would have cried over the small size of my own family, but there was none of that. I was, instead, treated to a glimpse of what our Father in Heaven wants for all of us. It was a vision of eternity. It would appear the "portion" she achieved in this life is larger than mine. But I knew, in that moment, that it didn't matter. In this fallen but brief world, every life is different.

There is no fairness here. Opportunities are not the same, but we all share the possibility of a fulness of that portion which we have achieved. Somehow, seeing the overflowing love on the stand helped me have a vision of what the Lord offers us. I felt the righteous spirits of that group filling not just the stand, but also the chapel; not just the chapel, but also the country; and not just the country, but also worlds without end.[259]

I wanted to take His Name upon me with all of its meaning and responsibility. I wanted to achieve whatever portion of love I could, so that someday I could abide perfect love. My heart sang in gratitude to have been given a role (small or large) in the plan of salvation. If our desire makes us ready to choose righteously and sacrifice with the motivation of our imperfect love, we can bring a portion that can receive a fulness. It is both an understanding of glory and a feeling of peace. It is the critical mass of love.

As a dear friend pointed out to me, "*Endless* is the name we can take upon us."[260]

---

259. Isaiah 45:17.
260. D&C 9:10.

CHAPTER 14

A Savior Has Been Provided for Us

*T*he plan of salvation is of such brilliant design that it is beyond the comprehension of the "natural man." Yet, our natural man thinks our own plan will do, or even be better. As Christ has told us, the beauty of the plan can unfold to us, but only if we trust enough to live it.[261] An experiment upon the word can subdue our natural man and make it possible to develop the attributes of godliness.[262] Then we can become the beneficiaries of our Father's genius.

When King Benjamin talked of this putting off our natural man, he said we could get all the way to becoming saints, not by ourselves, but through the Atonement of Christ.[263] That is because mistakes made before and even during the experiment leave their mark. They become part of who we are and leave us with debts to both the law and the people we may have hurt.

Inasmuch as accountability is a major part of the god-developing plan, the accounts have to be settled.[264] No matter the portion of our natural man we are personally able to subdue, and we must choose to do that, those mortal imperfections have to be taken care of. That is true both of the damage we have done to ourselves and to others.[265] So, since

---

261. Ephesians 3:17–19.
262. See Alma 32.
263. Mosiah 3:19.
264. 2 Corinthians 5:10.
265. Luke 4:18.

the opposition was necessary for our training,[266] the great genius of the plan is that a perfect being, who had no baggage of His own, would take care of it.[267]

I felt that I couldn't close this book without acknowledging the errors we have all made, both in the imperfect way we experimenters have lived our roles, and in the mistakes of those who come late to wishing they had taken the roles in God's design. Our Heavenly Father has provided a Savior for us. Amulek told us that this life is the time to prepare to meet God.[268] We can still use what is left of our life to work at developing within ourselves the attributes of godliness. It is not too late to choose to experiment upon the word.[269] No matter what has come before, we can still become saints through the Atonement of that Great Accounts Settler.

I love what Moroni says in acknowledging his own need for Christ's Atonement. He is pleading for his own errors to be a valuable negative example to those who come after him. We could all hope for the same.

> Condemn me not for mine imperfection, neither my father, . . . but rather give thanks unto God that he hath made manifest unto you our imperfections, that ye may learn to be more wise than we have been.[270]

We have talked much of ideals in the preceding pages. May we all strive for them, and may we all, therefore, be given a fulness through the Atonement of Christ, to whom we have shown a critical mass of love.

> Yea, come unto Christ, and be perfected in him, and deny yourselves of all ungodliness; and if ye shall deny yourselves of all ungodliness, and love God with all your might, mind and strength, then is his grace sufficient for you, that by his grace ye may be perfect in Christ; and if by the grace of God ye are perfect in Christ, ye can in nowise deny the power of God.[271]

---

266. 2 Nephi 2:11.
267. Isaiah 53:5.
268. Alma 34:32.
269. See Alma 32.
270. Mormon 9:31.
271. Moroni 10:32.

For the natural man is an enemy to God, and has been from the fall of Adam, and will be, forever and ever, unless he yields to the enticings of the Holy Spirit, and putteth off the natural man and becometh a saint through the atonement of Christ the Lord, and becometh as a child, submissive, meek, humble, patient, full of love, willing to submit to all things which the Lord seeth fit to inflict upon him, even as a child doth submit to his father.[272]

Let thy bowels also be full of charity towards all men, and to the household of faith, and let virtue garnish thy thoughts unceasingly; then shall thy confidence wax strong in the presence of God; and the doctrine of the priesthood shall distil upon thy soul as the dews from heaven.[273]

272. Mosiah 3:19.
273. D&C1 21:45.

About the Author

*E*ster was born in Seattle, the tenth child of immigrant convert parents. Her education includes a B.A. in English from Brigham Young University and graduate work in Ancient Near Eastern Studies.

She has served two missions with her husband: the first when he presided in the Canada Montreal Mission from 1987–1990, and the second when he served as second counselor in the presidency of the Provo Missionary Training Center from 1996–1998.

She is the author of eight published books and has written for the *Ensign* and other publications. Her work has been featured with Cedar Fort and Deseret Book. Her husband is James Edwin Rasband, a retired radiologist, and they have two sons and seven grandchildren.